DECA

Faith No More
in the 1990s

Matt Karpe

sonicbondpublishing.com

Sonicbond Publishing Limited
www.sonicbondpublishing.co.uk
Email: info@sonicbondpublishing.co.uk

First Published in the United Kingdom 2022
First Published in the United States 2022

British Library Cataloguing in Publication Data:
A Catalogue record for this book is available from the British Library

Copyright Matt Karpe 2022

ISBN 978-1-78952-250-1

Typeset in ITC Garamond & ITC Avant Garde
Printed and bound in England

Graphic design and typesetting: Full Moon Media

Acknowledgements
For my mother, Sally. My father, David.
My Fiancée, Carly, and my fluffy doggo, Simba.

Would you like to write for Sonicbond Publishing?

At Sonicbond Publishing we are always on the look-out for authors, particularly for our two main series:

On Track. Mixing fact with in depth analysis, the On Track series examines the work of a particular musical artist or group. All genres are considered from easy listening and jazz to 60s soul to 90s pop, via rock and metal.

On Screen. This series looks at the world of film and television. Subjects considered include directors, actors and writers, as well as entire television and film series. As with the On Track series, we balance fact with analysis.

While professional writing experience would, of course, be an advantage the most important qualification is to have real enthusiasm and knowledge of your subject. First-time authors are welcomed, but the ability to write well in English is essential.

Sonicbond Publishing has distribution throughout Europe and North America, and all books are also published in E-book form. Authors will be paid a royalty based on sales of their book.

Further details are available from www.sonicbondpublishing. co.uk. To contact us, complete the contact form there or email info@sonicbondpublishing.co.uk

DECADES | Faith No More in the 1990s

Contents

Introduction 7

1989: The Real Thing 14

1990: An Epic Year 27

1991: Indecision Clouding Vision 33

1992: Angel Dust 38

1993: The Dust Settles 55

1994: All Change 63

1995: King for a Day… Fool for a Lifetime 68

1996: Paths of Glory? 82

1997: Album of the Year 87

1998: Last Cup of Sorrow 98

What Happened Next (1999-2008) 103

The Reunion 106

A Selection of Setlists 112

Full Discography 117

Faith No More Followers 121

From The Author 123

Bibliography 126

Introduction

The story of Faith No More is not a particularly straightforward one, but, as proven time and time again, nothing comes easy in rock and roll. Very much a first decade of false starts and a revolving door of band members, Faith would eventually be rewarded for their perseverance in overcoming whatever obstacles were thrown in their way.

The core of the band has always been Billy Gould, Mike Bordin, and Roddy Bottum- even before the trio were part of the line-up, as strange as that sounds. Were it not for Gould in particular, the band would most likely have died long before Faith No More even became Faith No More, but the bassist was never going to let that happen. His passion and drive were a big part of the reason why the quintet is so revered by their fans and peers to this very day.

The early foundations of the band were laid in 1978 by Mike 'The Man' Morris and Wade Worthington, who formed Sharp Young Men and then added Gould to their ranks two years later. Having left Los Angeles to enrol at The University of California in Berkeley, Gould immediately went in search of a local band he could join instead of plotting his study schedule. Eager to pick up where he had left off back home, his early and short-lived bands had given him the music bug, and Gould's dream of touring the world was becoming impossible to ignore. Adding drummer Mike Bordin next, Sharp Young Men then changed their name to Faith. No Man – not that the name was to everyone's liking. Playing shows in the San Francisco area and creating a small buzz with their youthful exuberance, the four-man band would then record a double A-side single in 1983, having previously tested the waters with a three-song demo cassette a year prior. Before the single was released, though, Worthington would depart and fade away from the music scene, to be quickly replaced by Gould's childhood friend and an already accomplished keyboardist in his own right, Roddy Bottum. 'Quiet in Heaven' and 'Song of Liberty' showed a band on a mission, the post-punk sound and gothic nuances that Faith. No Man had created, drawing comparisons to some of the genre's biggest acts of the time – Joy Division, Siouxsie and the Banshees; and Johnny Rotten's post-Sex Pistols band, the slightly less rebellious Public Image Ltd (or PiL for short).

Gould, Bordin, and Bottum were still teenagers at this juncture, and with Morris being in his mid-twenties, the frontman was able to dictate the direction in which he thought *his* band should be heading.

Disagreeing with many of Morris' ideas and decisions and perhaps with a degree of petulance to boot, the musical trio decided to break away and follow their own vision for what they wanted to achieve. Ridding themselves of 'The Man', the singer no more, Faith No More was born. Electing for a guitar-driven sound (not that they had a guitarist yet), Gould acted as a channel for conveying Bordin's robust but pure rhythm, and Bottum's syncopated keyboard melodies, but they needed further artillery to really get their project swinging into action. Playing sporadic shows in between a relentless rehearsal schedule, the trio would call upon various local guitarists and singers to join them on tiny stages of whatever venues they could book for themselves, many of them taking the gigs under the clear understanding that their guest spots were only a one-time thing. Faith No More's first official singer of sorts would be a young but already troublesome Courtney Love. Before her rise to fame with her band Hole and her marriage to Nirvana icon Kurt Cobain, and when her confidence could still be easily mistaken for arrogance, Love's stint with Faith No More lasted roughly four months. Wanting the spotlight to shine solely on her and no one else, Love was already earning somewhat of a bad name for herself in the NorCal area due to her volatile attitude and reckless intentions. At the risk of being blackballed because of their affiliation with Love, Gould, Bordin, and Bottum decided to part company with the singer, also feeling that a male vocalist would be better suited to the style of music they were pushing towards. Now all they had to do was find one.

At least the trio had found a guitarist, though. Previously known to Mike Bordin but not particularly fondly, Jim Martin had played with the drummer in a local band that had also included a pre-Metallica Cliff Burton in its line-up, and it would actually be Burton who pushed for Martin to be considered for Faith No More – despite Bordin's reservations.

In the local underground music scenes of the 1980s, where everybody knew everybody, Billy Gould had been briefly acquainted with a keyboard player by the name of Chuck Mosley, a few years before Faith No More had begun. Forming his own punk rock band, Haircuts That Kill, Mosley would reluctantly become their singer because there was simply no one else – the constant comings and goings of band members something which a lot of bands can attest to in their early progressions; and while he didn't have the best voice, his raw punk rock energy had endeared him to many in and around Los Angeles. When Faith No More ventured to the City of Angels for a set of shows, Mosley tried out for the band and those few shows would turn into a full-time gig; his vocal style not necessarily fitting with the music he was singing over, but then again it was music that didn't really fit with anything else that was coming out either. Unable to relate to the flourishing hardcore punk scene where the likes of Black Flag, Circle Jerks, and Bad Brains were causing excitement and chaos in equal doses, nor the alternative rock scene that was in its infancy but had already seen the Butthole Surfers and R.E.M. make small impacts; a Mosley-fronted Faith No More was a complete oddity in comparison to any other act around in the mid-1980s.

Releasing their debut album, *We Care a Lot*, in November 1985 through Mordam Records – the first album to actually be put out by the once distribution-only company – a national tour followed in the early months of 1986 as Faith No More set to work in spreading their name and music further afield. In some places, it worked and in others, it didn't, however, the album's title track would somewhat elevate the five-piece through college and local radio airplay; its bouncing rap and funk rock fusion spreading onto alternative dancefloors across the country. The band signed to Slash Records later in the year, an LA label who had recently been sold to London Records- a subsidiary of the Warner Music Group. Guaranteeing wider distribution of future releases, it was a big break for Faith No More, who were already putting the finishing touches to their sophomore effort, *Introduce Yourself*. Receiving a $50,000 budget to record the album and with fewer time constraints and better-quality gear than Mordam had been able to provide, *Introduce Yourself* would therefore be seen by the band as their true debut effort.

Bringing in a respected manager in Warren Entner, who was already overseeing the career of Quiet Riot and who would later take Rage Against the Machine under his wing, as well as picking up a decent booking agent, Faith's next move in attempting to increase their standing would be to join the up-and-coming Red Hot Chili Peppers on their Uplift Mofo Party Tour of America. An intense two-and-a-bit month run of shows was generally deemed successful. However, there were already some cracks emerging in the Faith No More camp. Despite his charismatic personality and vibrant stage presence, Chuck Mosley was becoming more and more dependent on drugs and alcohol. During the Chili Peppers tour, Mosley and Gould would be arguing while Gould was driving the band's tour van, and Mosley would physically attack the bass player. The police were called, who, upon arriving at the scene, surrounded the van and ordered everyone to vacate the tiny four-wheeled box, and a broken finger for Mosley was probably less painful than the egos that were severely bruised that day.

On 16 May 1987, Faith No More's most important show yet was their *Introduce Yourself* album launch at Club Lingerie in Los Angeles. Representatives from Slash and Warner were in attendance, not to mention multiple journalists from esteemed publications such as *Rolling Stone*, but an intoxicated Mosley would let the side down when his less than inspiring performance ended with him falling asleep on stage – an act that would unsurprisingly make the headlines over the actual musical performance.

A first-ever visit to the UK was full of drama and fistfights, but it was also a trip that found plenty of foreign love for the five-piece, and it was the start of a relationship which would remain intact for decades to come. The revamped and fresher sounding 'We Care a Lot' received good exposure on radio and TV, the song written as a sarcastic parody aimed at benefit concerts and taking particular aim at the Live Aid event of 1985, organised by The Boomtown Rats singer Bob Geldof, and Ultravox's Midge Ure. Billed as a 'Global jukebox', Live Aid consisted of two simultaneous concerts at London's Wembley Stadium and the John F. Kennedy Stadium in Philadelphia, where over 160,000 people combined attended the day-long events to witness performances by the likes of Queen, Elton John, U2, Black Sabbath, Led Zeppelin, and Madonna. Raising money for relief from the ongoing Ethiopian famine, which was still gripping the country since 1983, Faith No More poked fun at modern culture with 'We Care a Lot', which included the darkly humorous line of 'We care a lot, about starvation and the food that Live Aid bought'. The overall sound of the song was what drew people in rather than the lyrics, though, and in the UK, it landed on the singles chart at 53. It is impossible not to also mention 'Chinese Arithmetic' at this point – an explosively brilliant song which revealed the band's early talent for writing off-the-cuff hard rock with dynamics that were difficult to classify. Tribal African drumbeats combining with chugging guitar and bass riffs, with subtle keyboard melodies and a resourceful vocal fusing punk rock, hip-hop, and heavy metal; 'Chinese Arithmetic' was arguably a more defining moment on *Introduce Yourself* than 'We Care a Lot', and it deserves its place amongst Faith's greatest ever songs.

Strong crowds attended the shows, which were generally booked in smaller venues with an average capacity of 200 to 300, and the band's energetic and heavy live shows went down a storm and received positive reviews. Unfortunately for Mosley, though, recurring critical pessimism surrounding his vocal abilities was becoming impossible to ignore. One review even suggested the band would be better as an instrumental act, a comment previously echoed in one of Faith's rejection letters when they had been searching for a record deal. People in the UK understood Faith No More, though, arguably better than those in the band's native America. In fact, it could be said that the quintet would forever have a more dedicated fanbase overseas than they ever would in the US. More fighting would occur between Mosley and Gould on that first UK run, and Jim Martin would also come to blows with his singer after he had rammed the head of Mosley's friend and instrument tech, Joe Ventress, through a hotel wall on the band's very first night in the country. Martin would actually find out he had broken some bones in his hand during the scuffle, but still, he managed to play through the pain and complete all the shows. Because he had taped up his hand and it failed to properly heal, however, Martin would have it re-broken and reset when he returned to America.

Mosley's final show with Faith No More took place in London on 24 May 1987. Beforehand, Gould had decided to quit the band he had worked so tirelessly to build up, but in a repeat of the Mike Morris coup, Bordin and Bottum aligned themselves with their close friend and bassist (as did Martin); and so there was only one other possible outcome. Struggling through a second UK stint which also included some dates in other European countries, further fighting confirmed that Mosley had to go – his departure officially announced on the first day of July.

The split has been well documented over the years, but Mosley's actions made it easy for Faith to get him gone, as their professional relationship had broken down just as much as the personal one, the writing on the wall for the frontman once the musical quartet had realised they had peaked with the moderate success of 'We Care a Lot'. In 2019, Mike Bordin told *Billboard* how the band knew it was time for change:

Once we finished *Introduce Yourself* with Chuck, we knew we went as far as we could go with him. We knew we had to make a change. And when you know you have to make a change, you just do it. We weren't at the potential that we felt we could be working at and exploring sounds in the manner we should be doing. We had to do it; we had no choice.

Roddy Bottum backed Bordin's statement by sharing his own view:

(Mosley) was an amazing, talented, crazy individual. But his singing chops had a very specific sound. He didn't sing in a traditional way at all. With Chuck, we would never have gotten on pop radio. 'We Care a Lot' was probably the height of what we could have expected in that regard.

Faith No More needed another new singer to build upon the slow but increasing momentum of *Introduce Yourself* and especially the 'We Care a Lot' single. Perhaps more importantly, though, the band had to change the negative misconceptions drawn from a well-publicised period of in-house discord, for which they were at risk of becoming better known than their infectious brand of no-rules rock and roll.

Not long after returning to the US, having put their European exploits to bed, a singer-less Faith No More commenced work on their third album – choosing to immerse themselves in music that would be just as hard to pigeonhole as that which had formed the content of *Introduce Yourself*. With the new material they were coming up with, however, the band knew they would need an extra special frontman if they were to ascend to the next level and not fade into obscurity. Posting an advert in LA magazine *The Recycler* came with no takers, before a singer by the name of Chris Cornell was approached. While they weren't fully established yet, Cornell's own band, Soundgarden, had already released two EPs and they had also recently signed to the independent label SST; and so Cornell respectfully declined Faith's offer. Somehow, San Francisco's *BAM* magazine (Bay Area Music) had got wind of the very brief discussions and they jumped the gun by announcing Cornell as the new frontman, a headline by which BAM had hoped to bring in one of their biggest readerships but instead required a quick retraction and a certain degree of embarrassment caused to the publication.

There were some positive try outs with prospective singers, but Gould and company could not hit the nail on the head as to what it was they were specifically looking for, and unbeknownst to them, the answer to their prayers lay 270 miles away in the small port city of Eureka. With a population of around 20,000 in the late 1980s, Mr. Bungle was still able to cause a stir with many of its inhabitants – in part due to a young and ravenous Mike Patton. Singing like a man possessed, his eye-catching performances full of deep gutterals and death metal growls, Patton's style was the exact opposite to Chuck Mosley's, and in theory, it should never have worked in tandem with Faith No More's music.

In 1986, Mr. Bungle's guitarist, Trey Spruance, had met Mike Bordin and Jim Martin and given them a copy of his band's debut demo, *The Raging Wrath of the Easter Bunny*, and when Faith played in San Francisco on the Uplift Mofo Party Tour a year later, Spruance and Patton met up with Bordin and handed him their newest demo, *Bowel of Chiley*. Like Patton, Mr. Bungle showed great diversity, from the death and thrash metal stylings of the first demo to the jazz, funk, and ska elements incorporated on the second, and it was enough for Faith No More to offer Patton the opportunity to try out for the vacant vocal position. More than content with the music he was creating with his friends, Patton only accepted the offer when his own bandmates pushed him to give it a go, so Patton headed to Frisco and sung on instinct to the brand-new music presented to him at his first audition. In 2019, the singer discussed with *Billboard* how he took the audition in his stride:

> They had sent me all these different tapes and they told me they were trying out singers and asked if I wanted to try out. So I was like, 'Why not, it wouldn't kill me'. But my head was in such a different place because I'd have to take time off school, even though I fucking hated college and the small-town mentality of my area. I just considered it a trip to San Francisco for the weekend, so I took a couple of the Bungle guys with me and made a vacation out of it. And then I went down to play with them and it was really cool. They had tons of material written already. It didn't dawn on me until I was actually doing it that I was auditioning for something.

A promising start made all the more so by Patton's ability to think up lyrics on the spot, further rehearsals divulged a blossoming chemistry that was only enhancing as each day passed. Although Faith No More took it upon themselves to find a new singer, they immediately had the backing of their record label when Patton was presented to them – an eighteen-year-old, good-looking, and unconventional rocker who ticked all the boxes from a marketing standpoint.

Mike Patton was in, his vocal extremities in some ways toned down for his new band's genre-bending musical template, yet his horizons broadened to even wider styles that his tones could synchronise with. Next, it was time to formally announce Patton's arrival, and Faith did so by booking a show at San Francisco's I-Beam in November 1988. A revitalised band fronted by a singer bursting with rampant energy and conviction, Patton's cocky stage persona created an immediate impact which went down well with the journalists in attendance. Less convinced were some of the band's diehard fans, labelling Patton a 'macho asshole' and refusing to continue supporting the group so long as the singer remained up front. Regardless, Faith pressed on with Patton in tow and, as excited as they were to reconvene work on their next album, the long-standing members knew it was likely to be the album that would ultimately make or break them.

1989: The Real Thing

The Real Thing

Personnel:

Mike Patton: vocals

Jim Martin: guitars

Billy Gould: bass guitar

Roddy Bottum: keyboards, rhythm guitar

Mike Bordin: drums

Record label: Slash

Recorded at: Studio D, Sausalito, California, December 1988-January 1989

Produced by: Matt Wallace

Release date: 20 June

Running time: 54:58 (CD and Cassette releases), 43:22 (Vinyl release)

Highest chart positions: Australia: 2, US: 11, UK: 30

Tracklisting: 1. 'From Out of Nowhere' 2. 'Epic' 3. 'Falling to Pieces' 4. 'Surprise! You're Dead!' 5. 'Zombie Eaters' 6. 'The Real Thing' 7. 'Underwater Love' 8. 'The Morning After' 9. 'Woodpecker from Mars' 10.' War Pigs' (non-vinyl) 11. 'Edge of the World' (non-vinyl)

(All songs written by Faith No More except 'War Pigs' by Geezer Butler, Tony Iommi, Ozzy Osbourne, Bill Ward)

> Things were changing; it was still the Whitesnake and Poison world, the new breed hadn't come around just yet. We were insinuating ourselves into the mainstream, taking up the charge from bands like Metallica. You needed bands like Metallica and Guns N' Roses to make it huge but keep in that punk rock energy. There was less and less nutrition and more acts just surviving, so there had to be some kind of change in there, opening up new fields where something could grow.
> **Mike Bordin, *Loudersound*, 2019**

Faith No More's third album was more or less completely written before Mike Patton's arrival, his lyrical contributions hastily added in just two weeks.

Basing his writing around the sounds and rhythms of words instead of their actual meanings, which often led to undecipherable sequences and passages very much left open to interpretation; his unorthodox methods allowed the final pieces of the songs to come together quicker than perhaps the band first anticipated.

Having already visited Studio D in Sausalito in 1986 to record *Introduce Yourself*, Faith No More returned there to record *The Real Thing* at the end of 1988- after first demoing the new batch of songs at Dancing Dog Studios in the warehouse district of Emeryville. While there, the band worked with Dave Bryson, who owned the studio and in just four years' time would be the guitarist and co-vocalist for Counting Crows – a rock band signed to Geffen Records and whose debut LP (*August and Everything After*) would sell over ten million copies worldwide.

The recording process at Studio D ran into January, thus beginning what would be the band's most important year yet. Becoming known for its live room with a 20-foot ceiling and tuneable acoustics, Studio D had also played host to prestigious artists such as Aretha Franklin, Huey Lewis & the News, and Earth, Wind & Fire, since opening its doors in 1984; the ideal setting for an act to utilise all of its functions in order to create music that would stand out from the crowd.

Matt Wallace first met Billy Gould when he produced Sharp Young Men's three-song demo back in 1982. Impressed by Gould's determination and musical vision, the two men remained friends and Wallace was always the first person to spring to mind when Faith No More required a producer. Working on both albums, which came before it, Wallace left no stone unturned in making *The Real Thing* sound as big and fresh and loud as possible. Roddy Bottum's keyboards were more melodic than ever, and the guitar work was brought further into the spotlight after Martin and Wallace searched high and low in trying to achieve the guitar tone Martin so desperately craved. Even visiting the world-famous Sound City Studios in Van Nuys to watch Rick Rubin and engineer David Blanco in action whilst working on Wolfsbane's *Live Fast, Die Fast* record, Martin and Wallace then returned to Studio D and spent three days painstakingly searching for the best sounds and settings. Before the duo began guitar tracking, each day, the two would partake in a morning ritual which started by playing Ennio Morricone's 'The Good, The Bad, and The Ugly' as loud as the studio speakers allowed. Once the song ended, the two men saluted the speakers, and then each other, and only once these things were undertaken would the guitar tracking commence.

Mike Patton's vocals exercised an assortment of styles and ranges that very few if any, could replicate, and during the recording process, there were times when Patton would offer up ideas to improve the songs, but his input was met with resounding refusal. Whether or not the singer felt like a hired gun in those early days is hard to say, but instead of taking issue with being repeatedly shot down, Patton focused on the job in hand, his jack of all trades voice box swiftly making him as equally important to Faith No More as any other member of the group. The core force remained firmly intact, though, as Gould's stirring bass lines and Mike Bordin's thunderous drum sections added a strong sense of familiarity, and for the first time in their existence, the quintet was happy with the finished product. An explosive set of songs had been created which perfectly flowed simply because there was no flow, each song different to the last thanks to a conscious decision to avoid repetition. Funnily enough, Matt Wallace wasn't so impressed with his work when he heard the final mixes and the album's overall sound, feeling he had overdosed on high-frequency EQ and compression. Virtually inconsolable, he even considered quitting music production altogether and finding a new career path, until Faith No More shared their delight at how grandiose their new record sounded. Containing lethal blasts of heavy metal, infectious bouts of synth pop, progressive and funk rock delicacies and even a bit of rap metal to really spice things up, *The Real Thing* was a treasure trove of goodies accompanied by a darkened sense of humour. Slash Records president, Bob Biggs, liked the album so much that he wanted it to be titled 'Album of the Year', and while he didn't get his wish, Faith No More would keep the name in mind for use further down the line.

Originally plotting for a March or April release, various delays resulted in the album not getting its launch until the summer. The cover art was partly to blame, the image depicting a liquid flame coming from a milky substance as the main focus, with an area of cracked earth forming the background. Slash Records created the artwork reportedly inspired by Harold Edgerton, whose 'Milk Drop Coronet' photo from 1937 was taken with a camera he had created himself which was able to freeze the impact of milk being spilt on a table. In the 1930s, an image such as Edgerton's was impossible to be captured by any cameras of the time, and his work would go on to be considered among the first steps towards modern electronic flash technology. With no input required from the band, Slash refused to add Faith's eight-pointed star logo to the cover, its reference to chaos and order through disorder not the kind of statement the label wanted to associate with both the album and the band ahead of their attempt to finally become a breakthrough act.

Further delays to the release were partly to do with the hand injury Martin had sustained during his scuffle with Joe Ventress in London, as well as an unfortunate but scary stage accident suffered by Patton.

Taping up his hand and playing through the pain to finish the final UK tour with Chuck Mosley, Martin had to have his hand re-broken when he returned to America as it had failed to properly heal. Before Martin's visit to the doctor, Faith No More played another show at San Francisco's I-Beam. Also acting as a music video shoot for the album's lead single, Patton was full of his usual uncontrollable energy. Breaking a tooth on his microphone stand early on was just a minor footnote because what came next could have easily stalled the singer's momentum before it had even got into full flow. During a rendition of Black Sabbath's 'War Pigs', Patton slipped and cut his right hand on some broken glass from a beer bottle, the persistent blood loss enough to realise something was seriously wrong. Five hours of microsurgery later, a patched-up Patton was told that due to severing the tendons and nerves, he would never recover the movement in the hand, but he would however regain full feeling. Oddly, the exact opposite happened, but in the years that have passed, the frontman has managed to become a fully-fledged left-hander.

Finally setting a 20 June unveiling for *The Real Thing*, Faith No More played a successful launch show at the Roxy Theater in Los Angeles the night before its release. With the venue full of label execs, radio and magazine journalists, and even big-name rockstars, a memorable evening was made all the more so when Guns N' Roses guitarist, Slash, and bassist Duff McKagan, joined the show's headline act on stage for a rapturous performance of 'War Pigs'. Early reviews of *The Real Thing* were extremely positive, and it seemed that the album was destined to turn its creators into America's next big rock band.

Ushering in a new era of Faith No More, *The Real Thing* opened with the relentless 'From Out of Nowhere', a pop rock anthem which found some people questioning whether the quintet had sold out in a bid for mainstream acceptance. On the one hand, such an accusation had a degree of validation due to the song being a deliberate attempt from Roddy Bottum to write a radio hit. On the other hand, though, it felt like Faith No More had been building up to this kind of sound for years, and finally, they had the experience and knowhow, and an accomplished singer in tow, to be able to reach their full potential.

Martin and Gould's heavy guitar and bass emphasised the work that went into finding the perfect sound and range that their intentions required, and Bordin's emphatic drum stomp further highlights the work of Matt Wallace in making Faith No More sound bigger and bolder than ever before. A hard-hitting but hook-laden song appearing to find Patton singing about a chance meeting with the woman of his dreams, the nasally delivered line of 'One minute here, one minute there, and then you wave goodbye' relatable to many an unlucky fellow to have suffered a similar fate. Clearly taking Faith No More in a new direction compared to the more one-dimensional Mosley, perhaps what is the most obvious thing here is that Patton sounds like he is having a lot of fun in his new band, as a certain swagger emanates from his vocals while he continues to adjust to the less vociferous requirements compared to the demands of performing with Mr. Bungle.

Given a polished gleam by fluctuating keyboard synth, 'From Out of Nowhere' would not be the song it is if it wasn't for Roddy Bottum – a self-confessed lover of *MTV* and 1980s pop music. His contribution is dazzling, with some of the melodies originating from 1983 on a track created under the title of 'Mike's Disco'. The working title of the 1989 version was 'The Cult Song', simply because it reminded Gould of the kind of song the English rock band would come up with, but in no way do the pop nuances ever become overbearing or, dare we say it, cheesy. At a time when keyboards were only integrated into rock music when power ballads were involved, Faith No More would be one of the first bands to prominently use the instrument, and the songs would be all the better for its inclusion.

If listeners thought they had the band weighed up after such an exciting opener, they had no idea what would follow next; in fact, it would become a common trend as both Faith No More and *The Real Thing* revealed a thriving quest for unpredictability at every turn. At a time when rock and hip-hop had seldom crossed paths, 'Epic' would tear up all the rulebooks in order to bring such a fusion firmly into the public eye. Swooning in with a triumphant guitar and keyboard salvo, the primary sound of Bottum's contribution was created by a Horn's Patch in an attempt to add a hint of *2001: A Space Odyssey* influence; but it is only when Mike Patton brings his rapping talents to the fore that 'Epic' reveals its true mission statement. Spitting confident passages over a signature funk-tinged bass line and marching drums bringing Queen's 'We Will Rock You' to mind, 'Epic' revels in a verse-chorus-verse-repeat formula where its infectious hook increases Faith No More's stock further. In no way is this a serious song; its recurring line of 'What is it?' providing the million-dollar question – the gang vocal response of 'It's it' not particularly helpful in providing an answer. In 1990, Patton told *Circus* magazine the song was about 'Sexual frustration, or sex and a lack of sex', and the bravado on show is certainly able to back the frontman's revelation up.

Gould brought the track in an almost fully formed state, the main groove contrived during a rehearsal session with Bordin and Bottum. Gould also created the keyboard coda, but by the time 'Epic' was completed, he wasn't so happy with how the piece had turned out. 'Epic' would become a fan favourite, though, its catchy combination of hip-hop and heavy metal a million miles away from the tracks it was sandwiched between; however, it did take a similar route to the band's biggest hit up to that point – 'We Care a Lot'. While adding in an effective guitar solo in the second half, an absorbing finale comes when Bottum supplies the melodic textures via a studio piano, and Gould the chords on an Emax keyboard – the melodramatic outro adding further dynamism to a song totally out of the ordinary come 1989.

When the song became a smash hit in 1990, Mike Bordin discussed 'Epic' with *Spin* magazine:

'Epic' allowed us to keep working and upped the narrative so far as crowds and people being aware of the band goes. That's fabulous but it also means when people look back, they go, 'Oh yeah, there's that rap metal band Faith No More who did the song 'Epic''. We just wanted to take the stuff we loved, cut out what we didn't. Nobody said you couldn't take the best of all different kinds of music and put it together to make something state-of-the-art. We did what the fuck we wanted.

'Falling to Pieces' returned to the pop rock mindset of Roddy Bottum, although the song's permanence would be all too brief. In many ways, it had 'Radio Hit' written all over it, the twinkling keys transforming the overall feel from the early heaviness of wiry bass and cymbal-crashing drums. Jim Martin's metallic guitar textures filter through, but on this occasion, they nestle lower down in the mix, allowing a catchy relay throughout its five-minute running time. Gould and Patton were not so keen on this one and it wasn't long before it was cut from the band's live sets. Lyrically, 'Falling to Pieces' is one of Patton's most honest entries, his new venture documented via lines such as 'Indecision clouds my vision', and the homesick admission of 'I'm somewhere in between my love and my agony'; perhaps referring to his transition of moving to a new city and playing in a new band, while leaving behind his comforting landscape of Eureka and his friends and bands that made the city home. Begging someone to put him back together, you get the feeling that Patton's later contempt for 'Falling to Pieces' stems from his soul-baring poetry. Regardless, this was another popular addition to the album for those outside of the Faith No More camp, with singalong capabilities and an infectious chorus to boot.

A section of lyrics would be used as an epigraph for the novel *Mala Onda* – first published in 1991 and reissued in 1993 with a snippet of Patton's words. Written by Chilean author Alberto Fuguet and the title meaning 'Bad Vibes' in English, the book examines the Chilean emulation of American pop culture and consumerism, as well as focusing on the psychological and physical growth of the novel's protagonist. On the demo recordings for *The Real Thing* and especially on 'Falling to Pieces', Patton would use a smoother and more soulful vocal delivery, along with spoken word passages. Fascinated by this alternative aspect of Patton's multi-faceted voice, where new sounds and ranges would be carefully revealed as he became more comfortable and confident, Matt Wallace pleaded with the singer to use these newly unearthed styles on some of the final recordings, but much to his annoyance Patton refused. Sticking with his nasally and adolescent contributions that fans eventually came to love, it is interesting to think how this set of songs could have sounded Mike Patton not held back on realising his full potential so early on.

If there was any fear of him or any of the band members holding back on 'Falling to Pieces', then those reservations were blown out of the water by the monstrous double-header that followed next. Turning the air sour, an element of Mr. Bungle is brought into 'Surprise! You're Dead!', a short but fiery onslaught of heavy metal. Faith No More had never sounded like this and it was sure to raise some eyebrows, infiltrating vicious riffs alongside a pulsating rhythm section. Patton leads the charge by channelling his inner Slayer – his deathly growls and screams full of bite and menace. Even the small rapping sections sound nasty as the murderous and torturous lyrical content comes across as unsettling but also slightly generic – much along the same lines as other 1980s metal bands such as Kreator, Death Angel, and the aforementioned thrash kings, Slayer. 'Surprise! You're Dead!' was one of the first songs put to tape for *The Real Thing*, its origins dating back much earlier when Jim Martin and future Metallica bassist Cliff Burton would hang out and jam together. A demo Martin created at that time would remain almost exactly the same once Faith No More had put the finishing touches to the 1989 version, and it would be one of the primary songs to earn the five-piece a strong heavy metal following.

While the first four tracks had their own personalities, it was perhaps 'Zombie Eaters' which offered the first real insight into Faith No More's increased songwriting talents. Told from the perspective of a young boy who is dependent on its parent, here is one of the finest examples of Patton's ability to create characters within his colourful lyrics. Opening with Martin's tender and pure classical guitar and a little hint of the mandolin too, Patton's soft and clean lullaby singing is a long way from what had been heard thus far, the ballad-like song given added early tension by synthetic violin chords and dissecting melodies. Letting the listener's guard down with dreamy atmospherics, 'Zombie Eaters' explodes at the two-minute mark with a pounding drum section and a deeply distorted bass line, before machine gun riffing progresses the song into a rather sinister period of devilment. The innocent but demanding protagonist makes a case for its helplessness through over-emphasised vocals of impatience, the line of 'So hug me, and kiss me, then wipe my butt and piss me' supplying one of the album's most unexpected but memorable moments.

Lasting six minutes but never outstaying its welcome, 'Zombie Eaters' took Faith No More's genre-bending exertions to new levels with expansive and multi-layered precision, cementing a strong case for the first five tracks to have comprised one of the best ever halves of any rock album released both past and present – if your preferred listening methods are vinyl or cassette. Side A of *The Real Thing* perfectly encapsulates everything that is great about the Frisco Five, where each song offers examples of their diversity and the weaponry they had at their disposal. Thankfully, the momentum remains in full flow for the album's title track, opening Side B with another ambitious and dexterous tour de force, which in many ways is more deserving of the 'Epic' title than the song that actually laid claim to it.

'The Real Thing' shows a band at the peak of their powers, constructed almost solely by Billy Gould but orchestrated by all five members into something all the more substantial. Clocking in at over eight minutes long and revolving around the side stick tapping of Mike Bordin, the progressive twists and turns unleash another side of Faith No More, as Mike Patton's resonant lyrics that are wise beyond his young years discuss feelings of euphoria and spiritual awakening. Each line is supplied with a hint of vivid imagery, describing 'The Real Thing' as 'The essence of the soul', and 'That golden moment', amongst others; similar to the 'Self-love' theme supposedly surrounding 'Epic'. Billy Gould's staccato bass is a driving force and the drastic tempo changes are led by Jim Martin's vast palette of guitar skills, all embraced by another wall of synth courtesy of Roddy Bottum. Extremely coherent and textured, the 'angel dust' possesses an everlasting power that, even 30 years down the line, has stood the test of time. It can be argued that Faith No More hit their pinnacle with this song despite its minimal mainstream charm, and over the years, it has frequently topped fan, magazine, and website lists of the band's best-ever tracks.

'Underwater Love' is another catchy and spirited number, yet it is more simplistic compared to those that came before it. Musically light-hearted, the same cannot be said for the song's intimidating subject matter, discussing relationship fears that lead to the insecure narrator murdering his lover. 'Liquid seeps into your lungs, but your eyes look so serene' is a disturbing enough line, but it would be interesting to know what it was that led to Slash Records asking Mike Patton to change some of his lyrics for this song due to the excessive darkness which came to overwhelm much of *The Real Thing*. 'Forever longing to make you mine, but I can't escape your stare' is further proof of the narrator's fears or exposure and obsession, with Bottum's Hammond organ the only part of the instrumentation that suits the track's morbid mood. Gould's funky bass tone leads over Martin's unusually subdued and methodical guitar, and Bordin has a more renounced drumming performance before Patton comes back in for an enhanced playout with the repeated falsetto line of 'Touch me from below, I'll never let you go' – once again delivered with a strong hint of alarming psychopathy.

The only slight lull comes via 'The Morning After', a noir-ish caper based on the 1987 Mary Lambert movie, *Siesta*. Following a woman who wakes up bruised and bloodied in Spain and has to recount her previous days in order to find out how she reached the point she is at, the movie's theme of sex and death seeps into 'The Morning After' with Patton's intriguing word creativity of 'When I closed my eyes, was it my siesta? Did I encounter a darkness stronger than sleep?'

Starting out as 'New Improved Song', the first incarnation of 'The Morning After' appeared on a cover-mounted 7" EP given away with the March 1988 issue of UK magazine, *Sounds*, along with tracks by The Jesus and Mary Chain, Head of David, and The Godfathers. The last track recorded with Chuck Mosley, the early version lacked any kind of structure until Faith No More revived it and gave it a much-needed overhaul. Bordin's staccato drumming leaves the biggest impression, but a less impactful chorus somewhat halts the charge. Patton goes all guns blazing on what would be his final vocal performance on the album's vinyl release, because the closing 'Woodpecker from Mars' ends *The Real Thing* with a spectacular instrumental.

Capturing the power the musical quartet of the band possessed, another heavy passage created by Martin back in the Cliff Burton days is modernised with some thrashy guitar pieces proving a formidable tag team with the drum bombardments of Bordin. Gould's slapping bass technique sounds good, as does the classical synth components from Bottum, who contributes some show-stealing violin swathes. An ornate and orchestral triumph, 'Woodpecker from Mars' would quickly become one of the highlights of the band's live shows..

On the CD and cassette formats, the album continues with 'War Pigs', a heavy metal classic created by British scallywags Black Sabbath. Faith No More had been covering the song in their live sets since 1987, and while their rendition doesn't particularly veer from the style of the original, they did replace the droning stoner guitars in favour of cleaner and more colourful textures. Recorded in one evening while the band was struggling to get a different song completed, Patton, Martin, Gould and Bordin got the job done in next to no time while they waited for Bottum to arrive at the studio. A song that didn't require any keyboards, Faith had further exemplified their credentials as a prospective heavy metal band with this enjoyable ode to Ozzy Osbourne and his Birmingham brothers, and naturally, heavy metal fans loved the cover, and they came to love Faith No More because of it.

And then came 'Edge of the World', the closing track and another which underlined that even at their softest, Faith could still provide an omnipotent darkness within their songs. Over a piano-dominated slice of jazz-infused lounge music, the nature of Patton's lyrics – which are told from the point of view of a paedophile – are even more unnerving because of the singer's use of a suave R&B croon. Inspired by the story of a well-known San Francisco supervisor who was found to be involved in a relationship with a fourteen-year-old girl, the daring excerpts of 'Hey little girl, would you like some candy', and 'I'll do anything for the little girlies' remain tough to consume; but clearly, Faith No More had next to no boundaries as the tracklisting for *The Real Thing* kept showing time after time. Eagle-eared listeners may have noted that with Bottum's keyboards not being needed for 'Surprise! You're Dead! and 'War Pigs', Jim Martin's guitar lying dormant throughout 'Edge of the World', and Mike Patton taking a song off to allow his bandmates to rule the roost on 'Woodpecker from Mars', it meant that of the eleven tracks officially recorded for the album, only seven of them actually feature all five band members. A rather interesting piece of trivia if nothing else.

Much of the second half of 1989 found the quintet bouncing back and forth between the US and the UK – a tour here, a tour there, and then the cycle repeating itself again and again. A five-day jaunt in England playing small venues in Birmingham, Manchester, Nottingham, and two dates at London's Marquee Club prepared the five-piece for an extended venture back home; and while their exploits proved rather fruitless in earning more record sales, a thirteen-date stint supporting Metallica during September was a welcome opportunity for some strong exposure to bigger audiences than Faith No More had been used to thus far.

Continuing to promote their fourth album, … *And Justice for All*, which had peaked at 6 on the *Billboard* 200 upon its release a year prior, Metallica took Faith under their wing for the West Coast leg of the tour. Vocalist James Hetfield and guitarist Kirk Hammett joined their understudies on stage for well-received guest spots on 'War Pigs' and 'Surprise! You're Dead!', respectively, while Mike Bordin and Jim Martin would return the favour during the thrash metal icons' set by assisting on covers of Jimi Hendrix and Misfits songs. Faith's popularity was clearly on the rise, the reaction and appreciation to their heavier material, particularly proving the band had a place amongst metal's elite, but still, their album sales and any commercial recognition seemed harder to come by.

For reasons unknown and some four months after the album's release, a single was then finally unveiled to belatedly promote *The Real Thing*. 'From Out of Nowhere' was the ideal choice, had it been put out at the right time, and although a music video accompanied the campaign, any initial interest was ephemeral. Directed by Doug Freel, who had previously worked on videos for the likes of Def Leppard, Vixen, KISS, and Poison, Faith No More's first promo clip to feature Mike Patton mocked the hair metal bands of the 1980s. Filmed at the I-Beam show, which would later result in Patton's emergency visit to the hospital, the frontman puts on a performance for the audience and the cameras as he dances and jigs while the rest of the band rock out, his childish facial expressions and vibrant energy clear to see what would ultimately lead to his downfall later in the evening.

Despite 'From Out of Nowhere' failing to gain any traction in America, it did chart in the UK at a respectable 23, where anything inside the

Top 40 could be considered a good result for any artist playing a hybrid of rock and metal. The UK and European single also came with two previously unreleased and unheard songs to tempt fans into picking up a CD, cassette, or 12" vinyl. Recorded during *The Real Thing* sessions but failing to make the final cut, an early demo of the first of the two B-sides, 'Cowboy Song', was one of a small handful recorded to demonstrate the vocal abilities of Patton to their record label. Opening with a sombre organ piece which turns slightly psychedelic when a cacophonous blast of heavy guitar, bass, and drum patterns truly fires the song into action, it is perhaps the suicide theme of 'Cowboy Song' that may have led to it being condemned to a B-side, which is a shame because it is one of the best songs Faith No More have ever written. 'You take the elevator to the top, the next thing you know there you are standing on the edge', sings Patton on a haunting pre-chorus, before the line of 'Just close your eyes and take the final step' reveals a helpless mental state of the narrator. A proggy middle section is again led by Bottum's organ patch, only outdone by a sublime guitar solo from Jim Martin which offers a touch of hope over the song's domineering sense of despair.

The second B-side, 'The Grade', is less a song and more an acoustic slide guitar solo which plods along for just over two minutes. More apt for the title of 'Cowboy Song' over that which preceded it, 'The Grade' is largely a throwaway track recorded simply to make up the numbers, its country sound at least finding the band delving into yet another style of music.

Visiting Germany, Norway, and Spain in November found Faith No More picking up more air miles, but one show, in particular, did provide a historic footnote for the band. Playing The Loft in Berlin on 9 November, the day the Berlin Wall came crashing down, Patton mentioned on multiple occasions during the show of the goings-on just a short distance away from the venue he was headlining, having been told of what was happening before Faith took to the stage. The muted reactions from the crowd may have been due to poor translation, meaning they would have to find out for themselves when the show was over, as East and West Germans rejoiced together for the first time since the wall was erected in 1961.

A US run from mid-November to mid-December saw out the band's concert schedule for the year and, while Faith No More had amassed a much healthier following, *The Real Thing* was still bombing, and Slash Records was close to pulling the plug on the band. Even so, *Kerrang!* magazine awarded *The Real Thing* their 'Album of the Year' prize, but it was little comfort because 1989 was supposed to be the year in which Faith finally broke out. In some ways, they had, but any early-year confidence had now been replaced by deflated cynicism. As 1989 drew to a close, Slash offered the quintet one last shot at salvation – by releasing a single of the band's own choosing ...

1990: An Epic Year

Faith No More's first outing of the new decade saw them opening for Voivod, on the Canadian thrashers' promotional tour of their fifth album, *Nothingface*. Chris Cornell's Soundgarden were also on the bill, their major label debut *Louder Than Love*. Having also had a release in 1989 like *The Real Thing* and *Nothingface*, *Louder Than Love* had elevated the Seattle quartet to the precipice of the soon-to-be grunge movement, its early foundations built upon by the fast-rising power trio known as Nirvana; and it was hard to imagine just how popular Soundgarden would become in a few years from now.

Although its sales figures remained disappointingly low, *The Real Thing* was at least recognised by industry bods who, upon revealing the year's Grammy nominations on 11 January, chose the album to compete in the Best Metal Performance category. It was a promising start to 1990 for Faith No More, putting smiles back onto faces that were fairly glum as the decade prior waved its final goodbyes, and now everything rested on the next single – the choice of 'Epic' being unanimously voted for as it was the band's favourite song on *The Real Thing*.

A music video was urgently filmed while the quintet was still in London at the back end of 1989, bringing in Ralph Ziman to direct the clip with a $60,000 budget to play with. Filmed in sixteen hours, edited, and then sent back to Slash Records, a typically chaotic and obscure video that was in keeping with the band it was promoting, the most memorable parts included a fish flipping and flopping out of water, leading to a handful of animal rights organisations accusing Faith of ill-treatment. In fact, an animal handler was on set and the koi carp was only taken out of water for enough time to get the required shots before being safely returned to its healthy habitat. Around the time of the video's release, there were rumours that the fish actually belonged to Icelandic singer-songwriter, Björk. Randomly given it during a poetry recital in San Francisco, later that evening, she later moved on to a party at Roddy Bottum's house where someone within the Faith camp supposedly stole the fish – a story later corroborated by Björk herself. Ziman s revelation of having an animal handler on set, who also brought along some bugs and snakes, was very much welcomed, and it more than likely eased a few people's fears of Faith No More being an unruly bunch of animal abusers.

Mike Patton's moves are similar to those seen in the 'From Out of Nowhere' video, as are his typically immature facial expressions, while the rainstorm setting with superimposed lightning strikes was actually created by the band being doused by umpteen buckets of water. Billy Gould hated the video, and the final scene where he walks away from a piano right before it explodes (the less said about the editing, the better) caused him further embarrassment, describing it as 'Las Vegas shit'. In many ways, though, the 'Epic' video perfectly captured the transition of rock music from the end of the 1980s and into the 1990s. It still had elements of hair metal clichés with regards to its visual aspect, but something new was coming musically, and Faith No More were unwittingly breaking down barriers for bands such as Jane's Addiction, Nirvana, and Alice in Chains to follow suit as alternative music gathered mainstream interest once again.

'Epic' was released on 29 January while the band was back in Europe. Their ever-increasing popularity in the UK served as evidence as to how Faith desperately needed more support from their record label, especially after 'Epic' crept inside the Top 40 at 38 without being featured on any major radio playlists in Britain. Soon, they were added to Warner's Reprise imprint, the label first founded by Frank Sinatra in 1960, and when 'Epic' began to gain traction on well-known radio stations across America, it appeared that Faith No More's luck was finally changing.

Faith may have toured with the Red Hot Chili Peppers before both acts became more established, and the band members may have even considered themselves friends – but that was before Mike Patton entered the fray. A rift between the two bands began on the back of the 'Epic' music video, when Chilis lead singer Anthony Kiedis appeared to take offence at Patton's rapping and his flamboyant dance moves. Writing in his 2004 memoir, *Scar Tissue*, Kiedis described how he felt 'Like I was looking in the mirror' when witnessing Patton's antics, much in the same vein as Kiedis' stage performances. On this occasion, imitation clearly wasn't the sincerest form of flattery. In 1990, Kiedis even jokingly spoke of his drummer, Chad Smith, kidnapping Patton and then shaving his head and cutting off one of his feet, just so the Faith No More frontman could find a style of his own. While words were indeed spoken, it was the media who made more of the feud than the actual bands did, even if it seemed like Kiedis was the one who couldn't let it drop. In 1999, he would take aim at Patton once again, but that is a story for later on.

The Real Thing finally entered the coveted *Billboard* 200 in February – some eight months after its release. Coming in at 188, the record then fluctuated over the coming weeks before ascending to 108. On 21 February, the 32nd annual Grammy Awards took place in Los Angeles at the

Shrine Auditorium, where the album went up against Metallica's World War I injured soldier themed 'One', Dokken's *Beast from the East* and Soundgarden's *Ultramega OK* albums, and Queensryche's pick of their 1988 *Operation: Mindcrime* rock opera, 'I Don't Believe in Love'. In truth, any of the nominees would have been worthy winners, but there could be only one, and that one was Metallica's 'One'.

'Epic' may have put Faith No More on the map, but it still wasn't performing how the band and their label had hoped thus far. Re-releasing 'From Out of Nowhere' in early April was a smart move, and within a couple of weeks, it had re-charted in the UK at 38 and earned the quintet an invitation to visit the BBC TV Centre to film a performance for *Top of the Pops*. First broadcast on New Year's Day in 1964, the programme became the world's longest-running weekly music show before it officially ended on 30 July 2006; but the 18 April 1990 episode remains one of the most memorable because of Mike Patton's obvious contempt for miming to backing tracks. 'From Out of Nowhere' was up to 30 in the chart on this day, and while *TOTP* dictated that artists should mime, Patton revealed the show's not particularly well-hidden secret by 'singing' whilst sticking out his tongue over portions of his recorded vocals. The defiance didn't do any harm as 'From Out of Nowhere' would peak at 23 in the UK – two places higher than the song reached upon its first release.

More European adventures were to be had through April and May, the core of the shows taking place across Germany; however, a double-header in London on 27 and 28 April were to be some of Faith's best yet. An explosive and well-attended Hammersmith Odeon show led to the band wanting to repeat the feat the following evening, but as the venue wasn't available, they shuffled ten miles across the city to the Brixton Academy. A 5,000-capacity music hall that in 1990 alone welcomed future and already legendary acts such as Public Enemy, N.W.A., AC/DC, the Red Hot Chili Peppers, and the Ramones, Faith No More added their name to a regal list and it would be a show they decided to record, with the intention of releasing a live album.

At long last, 'Epic' was firmly in the mainstream eye by May. The video was being played every week on *MTV*'s *Headbangers Ball* and the song was in frequent rotation on multiple major radio stations; the added record label support was clearly paying dividends. June was a particularly prosperous month as *The Real Thing* forced its way inside the top half of the *Billboard* 200 for the first time, while 'Epic' officially became a hit when it reached 71 on the Hot 100; and it would only climb higher as the weeks and months passed. An added bonus came when 'Surprise! You're Dead!' gave its creators some further exposure when it was included in the *Gremlins* sequel, *The New Batch*, providing a brief soundtrack to the frenzied live-action-comedy-horror flick.

By July, *The Real Thing* was shifting 75,000 copies a week in the US, and it was now inside the Top 20, as was 'Epic' on the Hot 100 chart. The single fared even better in Australia, and just as Faith completed a two-week tour of the land down under, the song went and topped the ARIA chart for three straight weeks. The five-piece almost scored a double number 1, but *The Real Thing* was thwarted by Van Morrison's *Greatest Hits* compilation, and so second spot was as good as it got for the album in Oz.

Elected to be the third single, 'Falling to Pieces' was accompanied by another colourful and bizarre music video which was once again directed by Ralph Ziman. Featuring flying fish (not real ones this time), stuffed dogs, and dinosaurs (definitely not real ones), as well as Mike Patton dressed as a bloodied surgeon at one point and then resembling Malcolm McDowell's Alex DeLarge character from Stanley Kubrick's *A Clockwork Orange*; whoever came up with Faith No More's video treatments certainly had a vivid imagination if nothing else. Strangely, the song mix used for the video was different to that of the album version, finding Patton's vocals more reserved and, in a sense, lackadaisical, while the instrumentation was higher in volume and therefore took a rather commanding lead. Released in Europe on 2 July, 'Falling to Pieces' reached 41 in the UK, and despite not receiving a particularly strong push stateside, it still made it to 92 on the Hot 100.

Before the month was over, *The Real Thing* had reached gold certification by surpassing the 500,000 sales mark. Celebrations for the momentous achievement were surely to be had, but Faith had business to take care of back in Europe, where some important festival dates loomed large. On 24 August, they played the first day of the Reading Festival in the UK, where if further proof was needed of the band's increasing popularity, they appeared higher up the bill over the likes of Nick Cave & the Bad Seeds, Jane's Addiction, and Mudhoney. In fact, only The Cramps topped Faith that day, as the festival came a little too early for the Frisco five-piece to be trusted with taking the headline spot. After Pukkelpop in Belgium, Faith joined Aerosmith, Poison, Whitesnake and others for the Italian and French legs of the Monsters of Rock tour, and with such esteemed rock royalty now regularly surrounding them, there could be no mistake that 'Epic' had turned Faith No More into major players in the rock world.

Capturing the electric vibe of their concerts and especially when performing in front of a passionate UK audience, the band's 28 April show at the Brixton Academy was released on VHS on 20 August. Recorded by William Shapland, directed by John Booth, and produced by Jessica Barford, the video contained twelve of the eighteen songs played that night, nine of which were taken from *The Real Thing* (only 'Surprise! You're Dead!' and 'The Morning After' were omitted from the tracklisting). Titled *You Fat Bastards: Live at the Brixton Academy*, the 'You Fat Bastards' heading stemmed from an incident at a January show at the London Astoria, when over-zealous fans caused a security barrier to give way during the band's performance of 'Falling to Pieces'. As security staff scrambled to assist in a quick clean-up operation, and presumably because they were restricting some of the audience's view, shouts of 'You Fat Bastards' rang out in the direction of the staff and from then on, Faith No More would use the chant as a rallying call. Remaining the band's only official live concert release to date, fans would have to wait until 1991 for the audio album to follow. The band's tour manager at the time, Derek Kemp, discussed how the Brixton show came about in Adrian Harte's *Small Victories: The True Story of Faith No More* book, released in 2018:

Brixton was an afterthought in lots of ways. We had sold out the Astoria on the previous tour, so the next logical step was to play Hammersmith Odeon. I put the Odeon on sale, and it sold out very quickly. I tried to get a second night there, couldn't get the dates, so (I) found out Brixton Academy was available, so (I) put the band into there. At that time, the capacity for Hammersmith Odeon, because it was all seated then, was about 3,500, maybe just a little bit less, and the capacity of Brixton Academy was around about 5,000. In two nights, the band played to over 8,000 people in London alone.

The belated hysteria surrounding *The Real Thing* peaked in late August when the album made it to the nosebleed height of 11 on the *Billboard* 200. 'Epic' became a gold-certificated single around the same time, while over in the UK, the rap metal anthem was given a re-release in September. Faring two places lower in the chart than 'From Out of Nowhere' had, it didn't dissuade the notion that 'Epic' was clearly the more universally popular of the two songs overall.

On 6 September and on the same day that 'Epic' hit a best-ever nine on the Hot 100, the song was nominated in the Best Metal/Hard Rock Video category at the *MTV* Video Music Awards. Amongst illustrious company once again, Faith went up against Aerosmith ('Janie's Got a Gun'), Mötley Crüe ('Kickstart My Heart'), and Slaughter ('Up All Night'); and it was Aerosmith who took home the gong for their David Fincher-directed clip.

A couple of small US runs saw out the year, the first of which had Faith playing the supporting role to Billy Idol. Once on top of the punk rock world, Idol's star was now diminishing and, because the support slot was a management decision and the pay cheques were small, the band felt an opportunity had been squandered in continuing their forward momentum, where they could have got on a different tour that was better suited to them. Music journalists consistently wrote of Faith outperforming the headline act, and those in attendance were able to attest to the reviews when, upon the climax of Faith's set, many would head on home without witnessing even a minute of Billy Idol.

Playing the Hollywood Palladium on 9 November as part of *RIP* magazine's fourth birthday celebrations, American rapper Young MC joined the quintet for an interesting rendition of 'Epic', and for 'War Pigs', Metallica's James Hetfield and the one and only Ozzy Osbourne hit the stage to assist in a pulsating set closer. The final run of 1990 was a short but well-received set of shows supporting Led Zeppelin vocalist and Rock & Roll Hall of Famer, Robert Plant, whom Faith befriended and spent a considerable amount of time with while on the road together. In a year that began with no knowledge of what the future would hold for Faith No More, 'Epic' completely turned the band's fortunes around. It may have taken almost a year for people to catch on to *The Real Thing*, but the stars had finally aligned for those responsible for creating the opus, and the quintet were now one of America's hottest rock exports.

1991: Indecision Clouding Vision

Faith No More swapped Europe for South America as their second home in 1991, and the new year was barely two weeks old when the band jetted off to Brazil for the second instalment of the Rock in Rio extravaganza. Taking place over nine consecutive nights between 18-27 January at the city's Maracanã Stadium, Guns N' Roses, Prince and George Michael headlined two dates each, while New Kids on the Block, INXS, and A-ha topped the bills of the other three evenings.

Faith played on the day of Guns N' Roses' first appearance, alongside Billy Idol and two local acts, Titãs, and Hanoi-Hanoi. The show pulled in an audience of close to 180,000, and if that was an impressive figure, it was nothing compared to A-ha's feat six days later, when the Norwegian pop rock trio broke the world record for paid attendance at a rock concert by performing to a reported 198,000 people. While the exposure Faith received during Rock in Rio was bigger than they could ever have imagined, their payment of $20,000 meant they were the lowest paid international act of the whole festival, but the quintet had certainly made plenty of new friends and, much like the UK had in the late 1980s, Brazil was the latest country to adopt Faith No More as one of their own.

A couple of dates in Chile in early February further enhanced the band's standing across the continent, and while they were still in South America, the *Live at the Brixton Academy* album was released to accompany the VHS that had arrived six months previously. Strangely, the tracklisting only featured eight live recordings, the only non-*The Real Thing* track being 'We Care a Lot', rather predictably. Closing out the album were the two B-sides from the 'From Out of Nowhere' single – the instrumental 'The Grade', and the vastly underrated 'Cowboy Song'. Despite the audio version of *Live at Brixton* not quite living up to its video counterpart in terms of value for money, the release still reached an impressive 20 in the UK's album chart, which was a considerably higher result than *The Real Thing* achieved at its peak.

It had been confirmed in January that 'Epic' was to be nominated for a 'Best Hard Rock Performance' Grammy, and on 20 February at New York's Radio City Music Hall, Faith would find out if they had finally picked up an award for their hard work. 'Epic' may have been an extremely popular song, but so was Mötley Crüe's 'Kickstart My Heart'. It still doesn't make sense how songs released years before can still earn nominations in later years, or why songs and albums can be included in the same categories, but Faith and the Crüe's huge singles had to compete with stellar full-length releases from AC/DC (*The Razor's Edge*), Jane's Addiction (*Ritual de lo Habitual*), and what would turn out to be the winning entry- Living Colour's sophomore effort, *Time's Up*. Faith wouldn't have to wait too much longer to pick up their first gong, though, in fact, they were the big winners at the Bay Area Music Awards on 2 March. A ceremony held by the Oakland-based magazine more commonly known as BAM and held at the Civic Auditorium just across the bay in San Francisco, Faith No More played a short set consisting of 'Edge of the World', their cover of the *Nestle* commercial, 'Sweet Dreams (You Can't Resist)', 'Surprise! You're Dead!', and 'Epic'; before claiming the Outstanding Group, Outstanding Song, Outstanding Male Vocalist, Outstanding Drummer, and Outstanding Keyboardist awards. It didn't go unnoticed that Bill Gould had missed out on an Outstanding Bassist trophy, something which Mike Patton ribbed his bandmate about on more than one occasion. Five awards was a very handsome sum but the high-profiled Musician of the Year and Album of the Year prizes went elsewhere – to Oakland's very own MC Hammer and his future diamond certified *Please Hammer Don't Hurt 'Em* album, which featured the annoyingly catchy and hugely popular hip-hop anthem, 'U Can't Touch This'.

In April, Mike Patton went out on tour with Naked City, an avant-garde project put together by the admired saxophonist and composer in his own right, John Zorn, and very much suitable for Patton's assorted and unpredictable vocal range. Taking their name from the work of photographer and photojournalist Arthur 'Weegee' Fellig, whose graphic black and white photography depicted the all too realistic and macabre side of New York City in the first half of the 20th century, Naked City performed an aggressive mix of soundtrack music, free jazz, funk, and hardcore; while some tracks ranging from ten to 30 seconds even verged on the brutal mix of metal and hardcore known as grindcore. Promoting their self-titled debut album from 1990, Patton came on board to fill the vocal vacancy left by Japanese visual artist Yamataka Eye, who can be heard singing and screaming on the studio release.

Zorn's mindset for Naked City was for the project to be an 'initiation workshop' to test the limits of composition and improvisation through a traditional band line-up, and the results on that first and at times paralysing album appear to achieve what Zorn had set out to accomplish. Patton's guest gig ran through to July. However, he did re-join Faith No

More for a quick trip to London, where the band performed 'Epic' at the third and final International Rock Awards in mid-June.

1991 was a fairly quiet year by the band's standards, though. *The Real Thing* had served its purpose and now fans were demanding a new album, the early wheels in motion as Gould, Bottum and Bordin started putting some early ideas to tape. A collective effort it was not at this point; however, upon the release of the second *Bill and Ted* movie, *Bogus Journey*, and its associated soundtrack on 9 July, there was at least an appetiser for Faith's dedicated following when the unheard 'The Perfect Crime' appeared alongside songs from KISS, Megadeth, and Primus. Jim Martin was even given a small cameo appearance in the film where, in one of the many bizarre and colourful scenes, he is introduced as 'Sir James Martin of Faith No More, founder of the Faith No More Spiritual and Theological Centre'; to which Martin responds by randomly shouting 'Station!'. 'The Perfect Crime' wasn't a new track, the bass and keyboard-driven rocker recycled from the first song to have included Patton at the writing stage – 'Sweet Emotion'. Effectively a demo of what 'The Perfect Crime' would become, 'Sweet Emotion' was originally released on a free flexi disc which came with Issue 258 of *Kerrang!* magazine in September 1989 ('It Goes On' by Balaam and the Angel was the other song on the disc). Containing new lyrics and a refined sound, 'The Perfect Crime' was very much in the same mould as the majority of the tracks on *The Real Thing*, but it didn't quite have the same durability as the album's finest moments and so it was shelved for the time being.

Another reason for an apparent lack of creativity in the Faith camp through 1991 was Patton reviving Mr. Bungle. Likely his intention from the beginning, and having frequently self-promoted his first band by wearing their t-shirts in music videos and TV performances during Faith's rise, it had already caused animosity with Gould and company to the point where throughout 1990, there were various rumours that Patton had quit Faith No More; and other rumours circulated that the singer had been fired. Such tensions would additionally rise when Mr. Bungle signed a record deal with Warner Bros. and received a $100,000 advance in the process. Patton had pushed for the deal even though he knew he would be met with resistance, as Slash Records feared he would not be able to manage two full-time bands, let alone two bands who were signed to the same major record label. In later interviews, Patton admitted to acting like a 'spoiled brat' by more or less forcing the label's hands, making it clear that he was there to do two bands, or none at all.

On 13 August, Mr. Bungle's self-titled debut album was released just as Patton was gearing himself up for another visit to South America with Faith No More. Promoted by Warner as 'Patton's seriously weird new project', the music showed a rapid departure from the demo tapes Mr. Bungle had produced in the late 1980s. Containing a mixture of funk, jazz fusion and heavy metal, combined with themes of sex, masturbation, and domestic violence, it was hard to imagine how such music could ever gain major label support, let alone any kind of mainstream appeal. Praised for the multi-dimensional structures across ten tracks with an average running time of six minutes, titles such as 'Squeeze Me Macaroni', 'My Ass is on Fire', and 'The Girls of Porn' may have contributed to the negative reviews that the album received, but perhaps the band's creativity was misunderstood at its time of inception, as both the album and Mr. Bungle have gone on to be widely acclaimed in the years since.

A couple of shows at the Obras Stadium in Buenos Aries, Argentina, on the last day of August and the first day of September saw Faith No More debut two rough versions of songs intended to be included on their next album ('RV' and 'The World Is Yours'); before an extensive tour of Brazil found the five-piece visiting Manaus (Faith were one of the first international rock bands ever to do so), as well as Recife, Belo Horizonte, Sao Paulo, Rio de Janeiro, Santo Andrè, Curitiba, and Porto Alegre; all in the space of 20 days. Before returning to America, the band made a quick stop in Japan at the start of October to do two nights in Tokyo, and their final show of the year came on the twelfth of the month, on home turf.

On the same day of A Day on the Green, 'Epic' was revealed to have been included in the action flick, *The Taking of Beverley Hills*. A movie which cost almost $20 million to make and didn't even recoup a million at the box office, the flop at least provided a small bit of movie trivia in the fact that it gave Pamela Anderson her first ever movie role, albeit an uncredited one, as she can be briefly spotted dressed as a cheerleader in a short scene.

A recurring Oakland one-day concert held at the Alameda County Coliseum, A Day on the Green's 1991 line-up featured Metallica, Queensrÿche, Faith, and Soundgarden. Worthy of being mentioned in the same breath as some of the biggest hitters of the year, Faith's success still paled in comparison to a flurry of albums which dropped within a few weeks of each other, where between August and October, Metallica released their self-titled and more commonly known 'Black Album', Pearl Jam debuted with *Ten*, Guns N' Roses released their double-album epic *Use Your Illusion*; the Red Hot Chili Peppers made further waves with *BloodSugarSexMagik*; and Soundgarden and Nirvana went global with *Badmotorfinger* and *Nevermind*, respectively. Surely there has never been a more historic succession of rock releases in such a small space of time – seven albums which in America alone would amass over 60 million record sales.

Blasting out the main highlights from *The Real Thing*, as well as earlier tunes such as 'Introduce Yourself', 'As the Worm Turns', and the live staple 'We Care a Lot', Faith No More added a third newbie to their set, 'Caffeine', to show people they were at least making small strides in working towards a new album release.

An almighty two-year campaign promoting *The Real Thing* was over and now the hard work was to begin. There was still time to reminisce at the belated power the 1989 release possessed within the mainstream when 'Falling to Pieces' was nominated for three *MTV* Video Music Awards at the 5 September ceremony. The track lost out to Aerosmith's 'The Other Side' in the Best Metal/Hard Rock Video category, and to R.E.M. and their arena anthem 'Losing My Religion' for the Best Art Direction in a Video; but Faith did manage to scoop one gong when 'Falling to Pieces' beat Neneh Cherry, MC Hammer, The Replacements, Seal, and Bart Simpson (yep, the cartoon character) to win Best Special Effects in a Video.

By the end of the year, one band member had gone AWOL, one was dealing with a crippling drug addiction, and internal friction was reaching untenable levels. It was touch and go at times as to what would come first – a new Faith No More album or a complete Faith No More implosion, and what should have been an exciting time for the band ultimately created a sour end to 1991; and the successes of the last two years were now very much a distant memory.

1992: Angel Dust

Angel Dust

Personnel:

Mike Patton: vocals

Jim Martin: guitar

Billy Gould: bass

Roddy Bottum: keyboard

Mike Bordin: drums

Record label: Slash, Reprise

Recorded at: Coast Recorders, San Francisco, California, December 1991-March 1992

Produced by: Matt Wallace

Release date: 8 June

Highest chart positions: UK: 2, Australia: 4, US: 10

Running time: 58:47

Tracklisting: 1. 'Land Of Sunshine' 2. 'Caffeine' 3. 'Midlife Crisis' 4. 'RV' 5. 'Smaller And Smaller' 6. 'Everything's Ruined' 7. 'Malpractice' 8. 'Kindergarten' 9. 'Be Aggressive' 10. 'A Small History' 11. 'Crack Hitler' 12. 'Jizzlobber' 13. 'Midnight Cowboy' (All songs written by Faith No More except 'Midnight Cowboy', written by John Barry)

The record company got really scared when they heard the finished album. That was the only way we knew we'd done something right. If they liked it then something would be wrong. There were a lot of worried faces before we started mixing.
Roddy Bottum, 1992.

Faith No More entered Coast Recorders in San Francisco at the end of 1991 before going hard at it in the first quarter of 1992 as they tumultuously completed their fourth album. Throughout much of their South American jaunts, the band had put their ideas to tape via Sony DAT Recorders bought by Matt Wallace, the producer giving each member their own piece of kit as they were unable to collaborate together while out on the road and on foreign soil.

Mike Patton was involved in the songwriting process for the first time, the results of his contributions easy to separate from the rest upon the release of *Angel Dust*. The main problems circulating around the speed, or lack of, of the album's completion appeared to fall at the feet of Jim Martin. Once Faith's A Day on the Green show was over in October 1991, the focus shifted onto the next record and with more than a degree of urgency – the demand for a follow-up to *The Real Thing* ever-increasing from both fans and record label management. In a cutthroat industry which never lets up on its unremitting forward motion, the need to strike while the proverbial iron was hot was imperative for Faith No More, or they risked being lost in the shuffle, having only just reached a level of notoriety.

Just weeks before rehearsals were due to commence, Jim Martin's father passed away and the guitarist retreated into a period of self-isolated mourning. His understanding bandmates offered to temporarily postpone the sessions, but an insistent Martin refused their proposal. However, when a rehearsal space was set up in Oakland as a way to make it easier for the guitarist to commute and join the rest of the group, he chose to remain in Los Angeles. Peeved that their efforts to accommodate Martin had fallen on deaf ears, Bordin, Bottum, Gould and Patton recorded their demos and swapped them amongst each other, and when their parts were done, the demos were sent to LA for Martin to add the final guitars. Because he had been absent from the songwriting sessions, Martin found it increasingly difficult to understand the direction in which the new music was going. A completely different sound compared to what was heard on *The Real Thing*, it very quickly became a huge sore point for the guitarist as he felt the band should be sticking to the formula that had brought them global fascination.

Martin had no problem sharing his discontent, and the snail's pace at which he worked on his demos meant that Billy Gould had to contribute a strong proportion of the guitar work. Martin later admitted that, having only earned writing credits on two of the album's songs, while it seemed he had grown uninterested in being part of the band, it was the stress of the recording sessions and not the music that had caused his disdain. 'Everyone wanted to be in the studio with me while I recorded', said Martin in a later interview, 'endlessly tinkering and fucking with me and fucking with Matt (Wallace)'. Before long, Martin made it clear he would only stick around and record if he was alone in the studio, so once the rest of the band had completed their work during daylight hours, Martin would go in and do his thing in the dead of night. It may not have been the usual way of recording an album, but with such a combustible situation at hand, Faith had to try something different, or the album wasn't going to get finished at all.

First opening under the name of Sound Recorders in 1946, the location was one of the first commercial studios in the city of San Francisco.

Renamed Coast Recorders when Bill Putnam bought the premises in 1962, he then relocated the studio across town and come 1992, *Angel Dust* became one of the first rock records to be recorded and produced there. Paving the way for others, the likes of Joe Satriani, Primus, The Breeders, Mr. Bungle, Neurosis and Counting Crows would later elope to Coast Recorders to record music, and most found the change of scenery highly rewarding.

If people expected *The Real Thing* version 2.0, then they were in for a huge shock, and it was perhaps at this point that many came to the realisation that Faith No More were not the kind of band that bowed to the desires of others. Knowing what they were doing was dangerous; it was partly for that reason the quintet refused to let Slash's executives hear the album until it had reached the mixing stage. When *Angel Dust* was finally shared with the label, there was a great deal of cynicism brought on by what they were hearing – an album lacking commercialism, an album tough to market; an album so theatrical and fragmented that it sounded like a completely different band to the one who had written 'From Out of Nowhere', 'Falling to Pieces', and 'Epic'.

The money Slash Records had earned on the back of *The Real Thing* had helped provide a bigger budget for its follow-up, but after the 'funk metal' tag had been placed around Faith No More's neck, the quintet was intent on ridding themselves of their reluctant branding before it well and truly stuck. 'This whole funk metal thing is really disgusting', said Gould in a 1992 interview. 'The last thing I ever want to be in is a funk metal band – we're gonna try to be anything except that'. And so that is what Faith set out to do with *Angel Dust*, the album title brought to the table by Roddy Bottum, who, during an interview inside Coast Recorders, felt the title perfectly summed up the accompanying content. 'It's a really beautiful name for a really hideous drug, and that should make people think.'

Completed by the end of March, *Angel Dust* was given an 8 June release date and after filming a music video for its lead single, Faith returned to the tour circuit for a massive support slot to Guns N' Roses. Promoting their double dosage of *Use Your Illusion* – both volumes of which were released on 17 September 1991 and took the top two spots on the *Billboard* 200 before going on to sell over fourteen million copies in America alone – Guns N' Roses also brought Soundgarden along on the European stadium tour; however, the Seattle rockers wouldn't come onboard until the second date, in Prague. The opening show took place at the picturesque Slane Castle in Ireland on 20 May. Homegrown talent My

Little Funhouse kicked off the festivities on this evening, having recently secured a record deal with Geffen, which was worth in the region of $2 million – at the time the most expensive deal ever offered by the label, and the County Kilkenny five-piece were being hotly tipped to be the next Guns N' Roses. Anyone who heard their *Standunder* album could see the comparisons in sound from a mile off, but their 1992 LP would be the only record the band released before they faded into obscurity.

Faith had warmed up for the tour by playing headline shows at Nottingham Rock City and London's Marquee Club, the second of which acted as the official launch party for *Angel Dust*. Humorously, they were billed as Haircuts That Kill, the name taken from Chuck Mosley's early punk rock band and most likely used without their old singer's consent. It was in England that Mike Patton showed off a new look, replacing his long hair for a shorter and smarter appearance. He now had a beard and an eyebrow piercing too, but there was also a growing maturity which only came with experience, and it would show in the coming months as the band started on the promotional trail for their upcoming album.

Very much a European vacation with plenty of spare time between shows, the tour visited Budapest, Vienna, Berlin, Stuttgart, Cologne, Hamburg, Hannover, and Paris; before three dates in England. Guns N' Roses may have been one of the biggest bands in the world in the 1990s, but they were also one of the most controversial. Notoriously late to the stage and often coming across as arrogant and privileged, the band's drink and drug antics, which came with their newfound fame and fortune, had appeared to turn them into rock and roll divas, and none the more so than frontman, Axl Rose. The first UK date was scheduled to take place on 9 June at Manchester City's then-football ground, Maine Road; however, the show was cancelled just a matter of hours before when Guns, who were still holed up in a Paris hotel, claimed Rose was suffering from exhaustion. Rescheduled for five days later, it meant London's Wembley Stadium kicked off the UK run, and along with Gateshead's International Stadium (as well as the belated Maine Roadshow), the crowds pulled in for those and the other European city dates were some of the biggest Faith No More had experienced up to that point.

By now, the lead single from *Angel Dust*, 'Midlife Crisis', had been released to radio and TV. They may have purposely veered off of their label's chosen path, but Faith weren't about to completely risk career suicide, and as they still maintained full control over their single choices, the band elected to go with a song they described as their attempt at

41

writing a 'slick pop song'. Certain parts emphasise such intent, but the variety of styles incorporated into four-and-a-bit minutes also reinforced the progression in their songwriting skills. With Mike Bordin's signature percussive snap from the outset, of which included a sample of Simon and Garfunkel's 'Cecilia', to the ominous string sounds from Bottum's keyboard and a one-note bassline from Gould that he described as 'a lesson in discipline' – despite its simplicity the bassline provided a durable backbone for the song, and everything came together upon Mike Patton's introduction. His hoarse and whispered rap-tinged vocals and counteracting cleans display an adventurous edge, making 'Midlife Crisis' an absorbing listen from its obtuse verses to its funky bridge, and on to its irresistible chorus, which was almost too perfect for radio. With a working title of 'Madonna', who Patton reportedly had in mind when writing the song's lyrics based on observation and speculation, the pop star in question was dominating radio, TV, and magazine covers in the first half of the 1990s, thus leading to Faith's unapologetic wordsmith creating an unsubtle social commentary surrounding greed, complacency, and false emotion. The memorable chorus line of 'You're perfect, yes it's true, but without me, you're only you' remains one of Patton's finest, and the theme of co-dependency first heard on 'Zombie Eaters' appears to be revisited here as the chorus continues with 'Your menstruated heart, it ain't bleeding for two'. Gould looked back to 'Midlife Crisis' during an interview with *Kerrang!* in 1998:

> Everybody's responsible for this one. It was a keyboard part that started it… it was a period of time when everyone was waiting for us to come up with another record and promising us the world. All we had to do is what we do, but the way they saw it, we were a little defiant, which I think the lyrics reflect in a way.

As with other songs on the album, 'Midlife Crisis' possessed its fair share of samples, its middle section even finding room for a snippet of the Beastie Boys' 'Car Thief'. A paradox of darkness and light and a stunning return from Faith No More, many predicted the song was just a taste of things to come – if only they knew. The Kevin Kerslake-directed music video also found the five-piece getting more artistic, and even though Kerslake was unsure as to the true meaning of 'Midlife Crisis', the video's theme revolved around torture – with effective time-lapse sequences and soft-focus close-ups, as well as additional shots of a religious cross, and choirboys, and a man seen being quartered by horses (an old torture technique dating back many centuries) which was a dangerous stunt that had to be done right, or the results could have been deadly. Near-psychedelic colour schemes mixed with impending doom created a suitable complement to the song it was representing, but for one reason or another, the video didn't hang around for long on US radio. The song did reach number 1 on the Alternative Airplay chart, but perhaps surprisingly, it failed to crack the Hot 100, while in the UK, 'Midlife Crisis' fared much better by reaching ten in the mainstream singles chart.

As the European tour with Soundgarden and Guns N' Roses rolled on, *Angel Dust* arrived on 8 June and the full results of Faith No More's latest work were available for the world to hear. To supplement the music, Roddy Bottum wanted artwork with a 'pretty' front cover and a 'darker' alternative for the rear, and after letting Jim Martin take the reins, the back cover, in particular, turned out to be far more sinister than what had been first intended. Mark Leialoha, a photographer and friend of Martin's, put the guitarist in contact with Werner Krutein, who would supply the stock photo of an enchanting snowy egret for the elegant front cover design. Almost classical in style, the vibrant blues and the album title presented in italics offered no hint to the content of the music included within the package, while Mark Burnstein's back cover photo depicting a meat locker with a hanging cow's head and a collection of strung up and skinned chickens certainly couldn't have been more conflicting to the grace portrayed on the opposing side. Bordin extended on the album's title during a 1992 interview, as well as how the disparate images on the front and back covers correlated with the band's thought process:

It has more to do with the band itself, the sound of the band, the sound of the record, the songs on the record, the title, and the cover, going from wide to narrow. The band, I think, has many elements, some heavy, some beautiful. The record is balanced, I think, between some things that are really aggressive and disturbing and then really soothing. The title of the record is something that if you didn't know what it was – if you didn't know about any drugs, it would sound beautiful. It's just something that seems beautiful but is horrible. The front cover is something beautiful, put it with the back cover and you've got something disturbing. That's what we wanted. The record cover and layout was designed by us and put together by us.

An energetic opening track is always a good way to start an album and 'Land of Sunshine' provided just that, leading off with a bouncing bassline and a raucous drum section. Mike Patton's vocals are instantly a step above the nasal deliveries heard on *The Real Thing*, but with new weaponry, in his arsenal, he is able to create a hallucinating thrill ride of bonkers storytelling – stemming from a sleep deprivation experiment the singer embarked on while seeking lyrical inspiration. Remaining awake for three straight days with only coffee, fortune cookies, and late-night television to keep him company, Patton used his findings to form a concoction of passages; the early line of 'You are an angel heading for a land of sunshine' coming from one such fortune cookie. His ability to create characters within his stories also allowed the vocals to meld and merge into those of TV hosts and narrators, and he even visited other areas, including the Oxford Capacity Analysis tests written by the Church of Scientology founder, L. Ron Hubbard, which were offered to potential converts to the religion. The fun and positive nature of 'Land of Sunshine' relates to the dizzying and carnival-like moments of melodrama, made all the more possible by Bottum's zorbing keyboard entries.

'Caffeine' continues Patton's sleepless creativity, where the first forceful and metallic guitar chug from Jim Martin allows his frontman to switch between deathly snarls and intense cleans. The dreamy synth adds a touch of relaxation, but with Bordin's heavy drum rolls, 'Caffeine' is more than a tad unsettling in its overall scope. A disorientated narrator begins to suffer from overstimulation as the song segues with abrupt fragments of dystopia, and when 'Midlife Crisis' follows in all its glory, it is clear to see how many a listener would have found *Angel Dust* to be hard to grasp during its early but penetrative three-song salvo.

With one of its working titles being 'Country Western Song', 'RV' changes the mood once again as the album's most curious addition brings Patton's strutting croon to the front – a style he had first adopted on 'Edge of the World' in 1989. To earn the rich country twang of the guitar, Martin added a harmoniser to his Fender Stratocaster, while a light-hearted piano riff nicely opposes the sarcasm of Patton's input. One of the clearest songs to showcase his character acting, Patton assumes the identity of a middle-aged and cynical trailer park resident, the dissection of the theme of 'RV' discussed by the singer in a 1992 interview:

In America, everyone knows someone who lives in an RV. These people are looked down upon, while everyone knows they're part of society.

These people are usually fat, watch TV all day, and eat TV dinners. 'RV' is almost a mark of honour to these pigs.

Faith returned to what they did best on 'Smaller and Smaller', where grinding guitars up the ante over keyboard melodies giving off a middle eastern vibe. The verses lurch along before the chorus explodes with some visceral death metal screams, but it is the sample-loaded middle section that gives 'Smaller and Smaller' its moment in the spotlight. String sections work in tandem with a percussion workshop from Bordin, and some native Indian chanting that would sound out of place on any other song by any other band, works well here simply because it is Faith No More who chose to incorporate it. An absorbing guitar solo also adds greater depth, and even though the band liked the song enough to include on *Angel Dust*, the mid-tempo nature of 'Smaller and Smaller' prevented it from hardly ever being performed live. 'While pretty grandiose in concept, it always felt too long and too plodding to even consider doing live', said Gould in 2012.

Amidst the chaos and opposing song structures, 'Everything's Ruined' reminded everyone that Faith could still come up with moments of easier listening. Powered by effervescent piano, verses seeped in melancholy are only upstaged by a soaring chorus. However, there is still room for moments of dissonance when major chords make way for minors. Revealing a financial disaster theme, Patton also adds a philosophical section which appears to be in relation to the pressures of record label demands, the carefully constructed boast of 'But he made us proud, he made us rich, and how were we to know he's counterfeit' possibly hinting at a nervousness to learn of Slash's response upon first hearing *Angel Dust*. One of the only songs to feature a full-length Jim Martin guitar solo, this standout track was just the tonic to break up the intense listening experience heard thus far; but even 'Everything's Ruined' could not prepare listeners for what came next.

'Malpractice' is one of Faith No More's heaviest ever songs and it may also be the most evil. A terrifying piece written solely by Patton, the industrial and nightmarish track is all about surgical violation – in this instance, told from the perspective of a female who learns that during an operation, she becomes addicted to the feeling of having the surgeon's hands inside of her. A fan of British industrial pioneers Godflesh, Patton took inspiration from the band as he thought up some crunching riffs and live-sounding drums built on crass ingenuity. A touch of Gothicism comes from the dramatic keyboards, an interesting middle section of triangle jangling offers a momentary pause for breath, and a short sample of Dmitri Shostakovich's *String Quartet No. 8* adds another leftfield dose of radicalism. As heavy as many of metal's elite in the early 1990s, 'Malpractice' showed that 'Surprise! You're Dead!' hadn't been a one-off dive into the depths of hell for Faith No More.

The groove-laden and bass-heavy 'Kindergarten' is another break in the stifling prowess of *Angel Dust*. A mid-tempo song displaying calmer structures, lighter guitar flurries, and unthreatening rhythm sections, Patton revisits the theme of age by returning to his school playgrounds of yesteryear. Lines such as 'Drinking fountains are shorter than they used to be', and 'The swings on the playground don't even fit me anymore' may not be some of his most profound, but they still manage to create a wry smile as they perhaps invoke childhood memories of those who are willing to pay attention.

For 'Be Aggressive', Roddy Bottum put pen to paper to construct an ode to man-on-man oral sex. Only a handful of people knew of his sexual orientation in 1992, not that Bottum's homosexuality was something he had ever tried to keep hidden. The first time any of his bandmates found out was during a 1986 US tour when Gould and Martin caught Roddy and a male friend in a passionate embrace; and six years later, the keyboardist was ready to officially come out and join a fairly small number of musicians having done so up to that point.

A celebration of sorts, 'Be Aggressive' is a colourful rollercoaster of funk and pop rock, the prominent Hammond organ, wah guitars, and swaggering bass, making this a song that is impossible not to like. The cheerleader chant of the title was recorded by a group of Patton's female friends from high school, and the rampant nature of the music refuses to subside during its near four-minute running time. With lyrical passages including 'You're my flavour of the week, I swallow', and 'You're my master and I take it on my knees', Bottum challenged Patton to embrace a new kind of character, and the singer obliged with a confident and commanding vocal performance. Full of youthful spunk, 'Be Aggressive' had more in common with a Prince song than it did with the hard rock bands of the early 1990s, but it was still one of a kind with Faith's signature groove unashamedly splashed all over it.

Next came 'A Small Victory', which included some oriental elements as Bottum's keyboard duals with Martin's guitar to produce some luxurious melodies. Full of samples Bottum had collected on the DAT Recorder given to him by Matt Wallace and later transferred to the keyboard, parts of Right Said Fred, *The Wizard of Oz*, sirens, bells and pulses are the nucleus of the song and provide its sprawling dynamics. Written about Patton's father – a coach who instilled in his son the importance of winning – Patton's lyrics reveal a hard lesson learned when he doesn't always come first; the pivotal line of 'It shouldn't bother me, but it does' finding a man adapting to a new mindset. Smothered in pop textures but still maintaining a rock edge, the mild and unthreatening composition is still ambitious enough to engage listeners with a sharpened focus in order for them to absorb the various sounds and layers.

'Crack Hitler' followed and it was another eyebrow-raising number that, even so late in the tracklisting, delivered another unpredictable twist to proceedings. Effectively a soundtrack song bringing to mind 1970s crime capers or a sleazy police drama, the mind-bending keys, siren samples, and a tension-filled springy bassline helped solidify a tight rhythm section. 'It's like bad, bad disco', said Patton of the track in a 1992 interview, but the sound and style was just another feather to add to the band's ever-expanding bow. Faith No More regularly entered a songwriting session after visualising a particular scenario, and in the case of 'Crack Hitler', the band's idea revolved around a black drug dealer whose consumption of his own product led to him believing he was Adolf Hitler. The song's opening sample almost got the band in some legal trouble, having recorded Iris Lettieri's voice while the quintet was touring Brazil in 1991. Somewhat of a celebrity in her native homeland after becoming the country's first female radio and TV newsreader, Lettieri moved on to become a flight announcer, and it was one of her readings which Faith used on 'Crack Hitler' – Bottum having recorded it while in Rio's Galeão International Airport. Told of her informative and calming voice being used on a rock record, Lettieri went out and bought a copy of *Angel Dust* to make sure it was indeed her, and once confirmed, she began legal proceedings against Faith No More's Brazilian label. Thankfully for the band, a financial settlement was quickly agreed upon for Lettieri's reluctant services, and the case was put to bed once and for all.

Barely involved in the album's songwriting, Jim Martin wanted at least one song that he could call his own, and that song was 'Jizzlobber'. All his own work and something he called 'Horrible and ugly', 'Jizzlobber' is welcomed in by the sounds of crickets around a swamp, and then Bottum's *Psycho*-esque keyboards only heighten the devilish guitar licks that Martin came up with. Full-on heavy metal, much in the same doomy style of Black Sabbath and Slayer, Mike Bordin's staccato drumming is another high point as he treats his performance as an audition for future gigs he would earn with other high-profile bands and musicians. It is Martin's work that deservedly dominates, though, even overshadowing Mike Patton and his lyrics that break down his fear of being imprisoned; his vicious screams worthy of the despair he would feel should he ever receive a long sentence of incarceration. The final minute of this marathon finds Billy Gould supplying a mournful period of reflection courtesy of a church organ piece, and again it is an interesting inclusion to a song so bloodthirsty for the majority of its existence.

Over the years, Faith have covered songs from an eclectic array of artists. In 1984 they added Van Halen's 'Jump' to their live sets – the first performance of the synth-heavy classic coming during Courtney Love's brief stint as frontwoman of the band. The *Nestlè* 'Sweet Dreams' advert jingle was a common inclusion well into the 1990s, and 'War Pigs' was the song to bring in a heavy metal fan base. During the writing and recording of *Angel Dust*, Billy Gould spoke of listening to a lot of easy-listening music, which is more than likely to be the reason why John Barry's Grammy Award-winning 'Midnight Cowboy' was covered and used as the album's official closer. The theme from the 1969 movie of the same name, 'Midnight Cowboy' soon became one of the most instantly recognisable themes of all time – created by a composer who would go on to provide scores for eleven *James Bond* movies, as well as award-winning contributions to the epic western *Dances with Wolves*, and the romantic drama *Out of Africa*.

An adventure comedy starring Dustin Hoffman and Jon Voight, *Midnight Cowboy* delves into the underbelly of urban American life. A culturally significant flick which would win three Academy Awards in 1970 for Best Picture, Best Director (John Schlesinger), and Best Adapted Screenplay, *Midnight Cowboy* remains the only X-rated film ever to win the Best Picture award.

For Faith's rendition of the theme tune, Bottum used an accordion to accentuate the lead melody, the feelgood instrumental similar to the original and its simple execution likened by the band to 'Elevator music'. Either way, 'Midnight Cowboy' provided an interesting climax to *Angel Dust,* considering all that came before it, its overwhelming sense of warmth and perseverance doing just enough to justify its inclusion.

Angel Dust was greeted with critical acclaim upon its release (especially by the heavy metal community), appreciated and praised for its leftfield complexity and for Patton's accomplished vocal performances. Debuting at ten on the *Billboard* 200 was an excellent start, but it wouldn't get any higher and within a few weeks, it had dropped out of the top 100 completely, and never would it return. In the UK, *Angel Dust* soared to number two and it was only denied the top spot by Lionel Ritchie's *Back to Front* compilation. Ironically, the two artists would have more than a chart one-two in common before long, when Faith's long-covered Commodore's classic 'Easy' would be added to a European issue of *Angel Dust* and released as a single just before the year reached its end.

Also recorded during the *Angel Dust* sessions but never released in any format, much to the disdain of many Faith fans, a short extract of a song by the name of 'The Shuffle', or sometimes also 'Seagull Song' made its way onto *YouTube* some years later. Containing an emphatic drum beat intro with some industrial tendencies from a stern guitar lead, the sound of the track was somewhere in between *The Real Thing* and *Angel Dust*. Lasting just under two minutes, the extract left fans desperate to hear the full song even if it wasn't in a fully mixed state. However, the members of the band have reiterated that it will never be released in full. 'We really don't like this one!' said Gould when asked about 'Shuffle/Seagull' in 2012. 'We don't always agree on much, but we do seem to agree on this… in our minds, it was a noble attempt but didn't really work'.

Years later, Gould would be asked by *Revolver* magazine how he felt retrospectively about *Angel* Dust:

Angel Dust for us was a dive off a high cliff, with no idea what would meet us at the bottom. It was challenging, stressful, and at times almost terrifying. It was a real and genuine period of growth for us on many levels, and the process reinforced a confidence towards our music that would serve us well in everything we did afterwards.

The European leg of the Use Your Illusion tour continued throughout June and during their sets, Faith included some of the new album's songs such as 'Caffeine', 'Land of Sunshine, 'Midlife Crisis', 'RV', 'Kindergarten', 'Be Aggressive', and 'Jizzlobber'. After the Delarock Festival in Sweden on 3 July, the tour was set to move on to Spain for successive shows in Madrid and Barcelona, but neither would take place and so the tour was brought to a premature end. The Madrid date was due to take place at the Vicente Calderon Stadium but with very little notice, the show was cancelled, when local authorities refused to issue a licence after they

found some structural defects in parts of the arena. Unsafe to allow a
mass audience in, the plug was pulled on the show and while it remains
unknown why the Barcelona date was also knocked on the head, Axl Rose
throwing a hissy fit could be as good a reason as any.

All parties returned to America, but they could still consider the tour
to have been a generally successful one, and it wasn't long before Faith
No More and Guns N' Roses were back on the same bill for a US stadium
run which also brought Metallica into the fray. Axl Rose had reportedly
wanted Nirvana to open the shows, the grunge trio's elevation to
superstardom cemented on the back of their 1991 sophomore monster,
Nevermind, which had spawned an anthem for a generation in the form
of 'Smells Like Teen Spirit'. At the time of the tour, the band's leader,
Kurt Cobain, was due to become a father for the first time – his baby
momma being a certain Courtney Love, and it was a good excuse not
to take the tour offer; not that he particularly needed one. Cobain had
his own issues with Guns N' Roses, hating what the band stood for.
In an interview with *The Advocate* in 1991, Cobain called Axl Rose a
'sexist, racist, and a homophobe', and he also refused to hide the fact
he strongly disliked the band's music. While he liked Metallica and had
previously said he would play with the band anywhere in the world
at any time, the only thing that would stop Cobain from backing up
his promise was if Guns N' Roses were on the same bill, and despite
Rose repeatedly calling Cobain to try and get him to join the tour,
Cobain never picked up the phone. In Danny Goldberg's *Bumping into
Geniuses* memoir, Nirvana's co-manager confirmed the reason why the
band refused the offer. 'There was a lot of money on the table. Kurt
really liked Metallica, but there wasn't enough money in the world to
get him to share a stage with that other band'.

Faith No More were called upon as the next best option. In some ways,
their position on the bill was very much a downgrade compared to the
previous tour in which they played just before the headline act, in fact,
the five-piece certainly ended up with the rough end of the deal in more
ways than one.

Guns N' Roses and Metallica co-headlined the giant tour, receiving equal
playing time so the two bands could split the tour receipts and earn up
to a rumoured $1.5 million per show. Both bands had their own private
planes, which transported them to the next city on the tour, while Faith
had to slum it on their tour bus and drive to the next venue, often leaving
the current show before the headliner had even taken to the stage, just so

DECADES | Faith No More in the 90s

they could get to the next venue in time. Some dates found the five-piece playing at three o'clock in the afternoon and they were paid a set fee, which may have been considerably smaller than what the others received, but it was still one of Faith's bigger paydays of their career. Ironically, the tour would be a huge monetary success for Metallica, but Guns N' Roses would only get around 20% of what they were expecting to take because of various reasons – most of which related to Axl Rose, whose over-exuberant themed parties after every show were a particular reason for the earnings being quickly swallowed up.

Likening the tour to a circus and showing their distaste for the rules (one of which was being advised not to mingle with the members of Guns N' Roses), the members of Faith No More openly discussed and remarked on their tour experience with various media outlets, which caused Rose to become increasingly irked. Before long, he would call Gould, Bottum, and Patton for a meeting, giving the band an ultimatum of either putting up and shutting up, or leave the tour altogether. Somewhat with their tails between their legs, Faith apologised for the upset caused and they continued on with the tour for a little while longer at least.

Unbeknownst to the band at the time, Faith had been offered the chance to join the year's Lollapalooza festival. From 18 July to 13 September, the quintet could have joined Soundgarden, Pearl Jam, Rage Against the Machine, Tool, Stone Temple Pilots, and Ice Cube; but without ever entering a consultation with the group, management passed on the opportunity – much to the annoyance of all five band members. Some of them would even admit in later years that had they been given the choice, they would have chosen Lollapalooza over the Metallica and Guns N' Roses tour in a heartbeat.

Starting on 17 July in Washington D.C., the rock tour of the year would have plenty of ups and downs for both co-headliners, who weren't exactly buddies, and neither were they appreciative of each other's music. Things went well for the most part until the tour reached Montreal's Olympic Stadium on 8 August. Metallica were on top form during a pulsating set that included 'Creeping Death', 'For Whom the Bell Tolls', and 'Welcome Home (Sanitarium)', but at the beginning of 'Fade to Black', things took a turn for the worse. Frequently using pyrotechnics to enhance their live show, Metallica were told that on this night the grates would be on the outer wings of the stage. What they weren't told by their tech was that those pyro grates were additional to the others already in place, and so James Hetfield felt the full force of the pyro during the intro of 'Fade to

Black', suffering second and third-degree burns down the left side of his body, both arms, and one of his hands.

Naturally, the band's set came to a close early as Hetfield was rushed to hospital for emergency treatment, and in typical Axl Rose fashion, the singer refused to take to the stage any earlier than Guns N' Roses' already allotted time. Inexplicably, most nights saw a two-hour gap between sets, but with an already frustrated audience missing out on a full Metallica performance, Guns N' Roses wouldn't arrive until three hours after Hetfield's accident – and when they did, they played an underwhelming show in which Rose was suffering from recurring throat issues. Because of this, Guns' set concluded early also, leading to groups of concertgoers starting riots both inside and outside of the stadium. Cars were turned over, fires were lit, nearby stores were looted, and police officers and revellers were injured in multiple melees, which were impossible to get quickly under control. Causing around $400,000 worth of damage, a farce of an evening had painted heavy music in a negative light whilst leaving a very bad taste in the mouth of the whole genre for days and weeks to come.

Mercifully, Hetfield was well enough for the tour to reconvene on 25 August, but as he couldn't play the guitar, Metallica brought in a replacement so Hetfield could focus solely on singing. Faith No More remained on the bill for another month until they were replaced by Ice-T's rap metal troupe, Body Count. Some believe the quintet were kicked off the tour after one too many run-ins with Rose, but it didn't matter because the band had a headline tour of their own to move on to. Playing smaller venues but knowing that all eyes were on them for a change, Faith took alternative metal pioneers Helmet along for just over a month's worth of shows before it was time to head back over to Europe and predominantly cater for their British and German audiences.

Three successive nights at the Brixton Academy and four in a row at the Barrowlands in Glasgow at the start of December were well received and, while in London, Faith were invited to BBC Radio 1's Maida Vale studios to join the *Jakki Brambles Lunchtime Show*. Taking part in an interview and Q&A session with a selected audience, the band also played live takes of 'Everything's Ruined', 'Epic', 'Midlife Crisis', and 'RV'. Their final show of 1992 took place in Doinbirn, Austria – just five days before Christmas.

Less documented until on the eve of its release, some were surprised to learn that Mike Patton had found the time to feature on a second album which was also released in 1992. Having toured with John Zorn's Naked City project the previous year, Patton once again teamed up with Zorn to lay down vocals on *Elegy*. Similarly experimental to Naked City and forged by an explosion of sound made up of uneasy moods and constant tempo shifts, *Elegy* was comprised of four tracks – 'Blue', 'Yellow', 'Pink', and 'Black'; all of which were arranged in the style of chamber music. Dedicated to the French novelist and political activist Jean Grenet, and also featuring Mr. Bungle alumni Trey Spruance and Bill Winant, 30 minutes of harsh soundscapes were made all the more abrasive by Patton's scarring vocals, some of the styles of which had been briefly presented on *Angel Dust* but now were fully on show without any restraint.

Three further singles were released from *Angel Dust*, or four if you include the promo-only 'Land of Sunshine'. On 3 August, 'A Small Victory' was accompanied by the band's most enterprising music video of their career. Directed by Marcus Nispel, the video was full of extravagant war scenes (filmed in a New York studio) containing gunfire and explosions, as well as makeshift references to religion in which alternative props were used to signify a cross. For the most part, the band members can be seen dressed in suits, and further interesting visuals only added to the well-executed baroque clip. 'A Small Victory' reached 11 on the Alternative Airplay chart and 29 in the UK, and included as a B-side was a cover of Dead Kennedys' 'Let's Lynch the Landlord'. The track had first been unveiled earlier in the year when, on 1 May, it was one of the most popular songs on the compilation album, *Virus 100*. Put together by independent record label Alternative Tentacles – founded by Dead Kennedys' Jello Biafra – the album of covers of his own band's tracks celebrated the ten-year anniversary of the label, and also for being its 100th release. Other bands of note to contribute covers included British grindcore pioneers Napalm Death, Brazilian death metallers Sepultura, and all-female grunge punks, L7.

A remix of 'A Small Victory' was also put out as a single on 1 September, created by Killing Joke bassist and keyboardist Martin 'Youth' Glover. A rock and techno hybrid, rumour has it that Jim Martin despised such a style of music, and to piss him off, Mike Patton pushed for the remix to be given heightened exposure. 'Everything's Ruined' then received a deserved release, and at the time, it was to be the final single from *Angel Dust*. Released on 9 November to coincide with the European tour, the five-piece played the song live on Channel 4's *The Word*. In the UK singles chart, it made it to 28. Surprisingly, 'Everything's Ruined' failed to make it onto any chart in America.

Because of the cost of the previous two music videos, there was no budget left by the time it came round to filming something for 'Everything's Ruined'. In response, Kevin Kerslake directed an intentionally cheap-looking clip in which Faith can be seen superimposed over blue-screened stock footage ranging from wildlife to sports, and from teleshopping to family activities; the funniest moment coming when the band pretends to act scared by a giant tortoise peering over them. After the sublime video for 'A Small Victory', 'Everything's Ruined' returned to the comedic and haphazard side of the band, and while much of Faith No More's videography has always been taken with a pinch of salt, this one, unfortunately, neutralised the impact of the quite brilliant song it was promoting.

The beginning of 1992 had been quite fractious for the quintet and the disparate sounds that revealed themselves on *Angel Dust* emphasised that, but the album was still able to cement Faith No More as a unique act who, when able to come together as a cohesive unit, could bring highly impressionable songs to the table whether they possessed mainstream appeal or not. *Angel Dust* may not have lit up the charts like their management and record label had hoped, but Faith were not in the music business to specifically earn such recognition. Their fourth opus has gone on to sell over three million copies worldwide, the songs providing a lasting legacy while also underlining Faith No More's true value to the continued evolution of rock music throughout the first half of the decade.

1993: The Dust Settles

1993 began with a bang when Faith scored an unexpected hit in the UK singles chart. Their cover of 'War Pigs' had long been a popular staple in live sets, the Black Sabbath classic often left until last on the setlist and sending audiences home happy, especially the metalheads who were probably only in attendance to hear that one song. To spite those who had become expectant of a small dose of heavy metal, Faith started to re-place 'War Pigs' with their take on the Commodores' pop soul hit, 'Easy'. The two songs could not have been more disparate. Deciding to record the song during the *Angel Dust* sessions but having no intention of doing anything with it, 'Easy' was first included on a European issue of the album without the band's knowledge. Then it was decided it should be re-leased in the UK as a double A-side single along with 'Be Aggressive', just two days after Christmas in 1992. It wasn't until two weeks into the new year, however, when 'Easy' gained traction, and within the blink of an eye, the song rose to number three in the chart; the only songs above it being 'Exterminate' by Snap! and Niki Harris, and Whitney Houston's cover of 'I Will Always Love You', which was celebrating its tenth straight week at number one.

In 1995, Roddy Bottum discussed how 'Easy' first etched itself into Faith's setlists and then why they later put it to tape:

Recording it was probably Billy's idea. Our fans would scream for 'War Pigs', but being the kind of band we are, never wanting to be pigeonholed, never wanting to give people what they expect, and as a way of balancing things up… when people yelled for the cover song, we gave them a different cover. The flip side of the coin. Then because we liked how we played it and the way Mike sang it, we recorded it for a B-side. Then the record company had a brilliant idea to put it out as an A-side, and we made a really nice video.

On 13 January, Faith performed 'Easy' and 'Midlife Crisis' on *The Tonight Show with Jay Leno* at NBC Studios in Burbank, California. Acting as the musical guest, interviewees on that particular episode were American actor and comedian Craig T. Nelson, Cuban American jazz artist Arturo Sandoval, and Italian-American actress Marisa Tomei. Two days later, the quintet began a three-week tour of America where they took along the alt rockers Babes in Toyland, and the stoner heavies, Kyuss.

Angel Dust earned a Grammy nomination in February in the Best Hard Rock Performance category, where they were pitted against an all-star cast of the Red Hot Chili Peppers ('Give It Away'), Alice in Chains (*Dirt*), Guns N' Roses ('Live and Let Die'), Nirvana ('Smells Like Teen Spirit'), and Pearl Jam ('Jeremy'). As with all their Grammy nods, Faith No More were huge underdogs and this time was no different. Every nomination could have made a strong case to be the winner, and this time it was Faith's rivals of sorts, the Chili Peppers, who took home the award for the funk-heavy highlight of the band's fifth album, *BloodSugarSexMagik*.

February also saw the release of the band's first video compilation. Arriving in the UK on the second day of the month and three weeks later in America, the eccentrically titled *Video Croissant* featured all the music videos of the singles from *The Real Thing* and *Angel Dust*, as well as the Chuck Mosley-era clips for 'We Care a Lot' and 'Anne's Song'. A live recording of 'Caffeine' which was filmed for the *Hangin' with MTV* show, was also included, while behind-the-scenes footage from the 1991 Brazilian tour and interview snippets were used to supply further content. At a time when music videos came and went from TV rather quickly and there was no internet and the likes of *YouTube* to store them on demand, *Video Croissant* proved to be a popular release for hardcore fans of Faith No More; but had it been around in today's climate, it would likely have been nothing more than a collection piece for the purists.

On the back of the success that 'Easy' had gained in the UK, Faith's management decided to put the song out in America to see if it would grab similar attention on home turf. Three different versions of the track were released and received in various parts of the world, two of which had progressions of the song's original title. For most of the European issues, 'I'm Easy' featured an added voice-over from Mike Patton during the intro, while 'Easy (Cooler Version)' differed to the others by having additional string and horn arrangements. The third and simpler 'Easy' contained neither of the above and was primarily released in the Far East.

According to online records, Faith No More first covered 'Easy' in April 1990 during a show at Nottingham Rock City. To date, statistics compiled by *Setlist.fm*, which is a website that allows and relies on concertgoers to upload the setlists of shows they attend, list 'Easy' as the third most-played song by the band behind 'Epic' and 'We Care a Lot'. The list may not be authenticated, but it is likely that the higher-ranking songs aren't too far off being correct.

Shooting a luxurious and indulgent music video and directed by Barry McGuire, in which live footage is interspersed with scenes filmed in a swanky hotel where the band members are seen mixing with pretty women, transvestites, and er, flamingos, the video strongly suited the song's rich verve; and judging by the amount of champagne consumed within the four-minute clip, a good time appeared to be had by all during its filming. Billy Gould liked the video too, when speaking to *Billboard* in 1993, 'Of all the videos we've done, it probably has our personality the most. People can find something sympathetic through a weird medium. It's almost touching that this transvestite is sitting there drinking champagne while Mike is singing'.

Releasing 'Easy' with 'Be Aggressive' was an interesting choice – one song being a ballad which reveals lovesick tendencies, and the other discussing oral sex between two men, the opposite nature of the songs was likely the reason why Faith chose to put them together in the first place. 'Be Aggressive' may also have been an instantly catchy and infectious funk/pop/rock song and musically, it made for an ideal single choice, but it was 'Easy' which had the most promotion and exposure, and so it was unsurprising that any chart success was down that song and not the other. Even Lionel Ritchie approved of Faith's rendition, admitting a while later that he was flattered the band chose to cover the song, and that he 'loved it'.

For American audiences, 'Easy' got its release on 3 April when it led the four-track EP, *Songs to Make Love To*. Using the same cover art as for 'Everything's Ruined' (depicting a rhinoceros mounting another), *Songs to Make Love to* consisted of the 'Cooler Version' of 'Easy', 'Das Schutzenfest', 'Midnight Cowboy'; and the Dead Kennedys' cover, 'Let's Lynch the Landlord'. Sang in comedic German by Patton, the previously unheard 'Das Schutzenfest' was a polka track where the lyrics (written by a friend of the band) tell the story of the narrator meeting a Bavarian woman at a shooting party and then making love to her in a pig trough. Not ones to show an overly romantic side, this was probably as close as the listener would get to hearing Faith No More in a lovey-dovey kind of mood in the first half of the 1990s, the line of 'The armpit was fresh and fragrant as summer morning' as silly and as cheesy as you will ever hear. On the back of the release, 'Easy' reached 58 on *Billboard*'s Hot 100, and as the heavy music scene changed in the US over the next few years, it would be the Commodores cover that gave Faith No More their last entry on the esteemed American singles chart.

A handful of shows throughout April found the band visiting Mexico, Honolulu, and Guam for one-offs before four shows in Japan preceded an intense two-week tour of Australia. On the day of the first concert, which was held in Canberra, Faith were welcomed onto the *Hey It's Saturday* TV show for a special performance of 'Easy', and as they chalked off successful visits to Brisbane, Newcastle, Wollongong, Perth, Adelaide, Hobart, Melbourne, and Sydney, 'Easy' went to number 1 on the ARIA singles chart for two consecutive weeks.

A week in New Zealand followed before the European festival season sprang into action and Faith arrived just in time for Rock AM Ring in Germany on 29 May. Headlined by Aussie favourites, INXS, and with Leonard Cohen and The Cranberries also on the bill at the Nürburgring, it was a decent festival for Faith to get onto, even if the line-up seemed a little all over the place. Thanks to much of the *Angel Dust* material included in their set, the Frisco five would be one of the heavier acts to take to the stage that day. Moving on to Berlin Rocks on 4 June, a mouth-watering line-up much more suited to Faith's current style combined the crossover thrash of Anthrax and the Suicidal Tendencies, the raw punk rock attitude of Iggy Pop, and the up-and-coming rap metal quartet, Rage Against the Machine; making sure all types of hard rock and heavy metal was represented throughout the day. Faith still managed to incorporate the slow burners of 'RV', 'Edge of the World', and 'Easy' into their setlist, but 'Surprise! You're Dead!', 'Woodpecker from Mars', and 'Jizzlobber' counteracted the balance to provide extra weight and heavy muscle.

Speaking of heavy – performing a completely different style of music than people had been used to hearing from Billy Gould, the bassist had also been playing in the grindcore/death metal outfit Brujeria since 1989, and 1993 saw the band issue their debut album. A fascinatingly violent supergroup of sorts where the members went under pseudonyms and portrayed themselves as Latino drug dealers, the name 'Brujeria' translated into English meant 'Witchcraft'. Representing the Latino and Chicano communities, other musicians who were part of the ensemble in 1993 included the Fear Factory duo of Dino Cazares and Raymond Herrera, plus Napalm Death's Shane Embury. After releasing a couple of singles in 1990 and 1992, *Matando Güeros* was distributed via Roadrunner Records on 6 July, and the record touched on controversial topics in Mexico such as drug trafficking, satanic rituals, sexuality and anti-Americanism; the last of which is openly and vividly discussed in the title track where the narrator talks of revenge killings against Americans for the mistreatment of indigenous Mexicans.

The combination of grindcore and brutal death metal which Brujeria performed meant they were one of the heaviest bands around in 1993, but their initial exposure was limited due to the album's cover art – which showed the severed head of a drug dealer and thus contributing to the album being banned in multiple countries. Regardless, *Matando Güeros*, which basically means to kill white people, was a commended release, and to hear Gould's bass and additional guitar work on songs that in English meant 'Fuckload of Cum' and 'Molesting Dead Children' seemed lightyears away from the catchy stomps of other songs he was part of creating around that time.

The Out in the Green fest in Frauenfeld, Switzerland, on 9 July found the five-piece once again playing on a more alternative bill of artists on the first day of the three-day event, joining Chris Isaak (who doesn't know 'Wicked Game'?), Lenny Kravitz, The Black Crowes, and Uriah Heep. Elsewhere in the early summer, Faith performed in Slovakia, Poland, Russia, Sweden, Denmark, Norway, Portugal, Estonia, and Belgium; before making one final stop – in England.

Between 16-18 July, Phoenix Festival took place at Marston Airfield in Stratford-upon-Avon, a medieval town and the birthplace of William Shakespeare, some 40 miles outside of Birmingham. In its debut year and set up to offer music lovers an alternate option to the more popular Glastonbury and Reading festivals, Sonic Youth headlined the Friday, Faith headlined Saturday, and The Black Crowes closed the event on the Sunday evening. With a line-up worthy of competing with Reading in particular, which tended to feature slightly heavier acts compared to what could be found on a Glastonbury bill, Phoenix started off with a bang by welcoming Courtney Love's Hole, alternative metal pioneers Helmet, punk rock kings Bad Religion, British indie rockers the Manic Street Preachers, and the hip-hop royalty of Cypress Hill; amongst a long list of acts to play across the whole weekend. The event would also play host to Faith No More's final show of 1993, where they performed a twenty-one-song set that provided a little bit of everything, from the Mosley-era 'Chinese Arithmetic', 'Mark Bowen', and 'The Crab Song', to 'Jizzlobber', 'Be Aggressive', and 'Zombie Eaters'; before closing out with 'Epic'. No one knew it at the time, but it would also be the last show Jim Martin would ever play with the band.

It was obvious that from the early stages of the *Angel Dust* sessions that a chasm was forming between the guitarist and rest of the band, and audiences were able to perceive this on many an occasion during live performances. At times Martin would stand on his own on one side of the stage, cast out in the cold and merely there to play the guitar on many songs he had little or no involvement in bringing to life. His bandmates would regularly chastise him, poking fun at him and therefore forging an even bigger divide, a four-on-one handicap which at times became uneasy to witness and the situation would only increase until breaking point was reached.

When Faith returned to America, Martin went AWOL, and the final death knell came when he refused to be part of a collaboration with Boo-Yaa T.R.I.B.E. for the *Judgement Night* movie soundtrack. An action thriller directed by Stephen Hopkins and distributed by Universal Pictures, *Judgement Night* starred Emilio Estevez, Cuba Gooding Jr, Jeremy Piven, Stephen Dorff, and Denis Leary and told the story of a group of friends who travel to Chicago to watch a boxing match. At a standstill on a freeway, the friends decide to take the offramp and cut through a dilapidated and dangerous neighbourhood, and upon witnessing a murder, survival becomes the name of the game when the friends become the targets of a vicious gang. Very much a cult soundtrack, then-music producer and band manager Happy Walters decided to assemble an all-star cast of rock and rap artists to come together, his idea forged upon capitalising on the flourishing popularity of the rap rock hybrid, which ironically had a little something to do with a song by the name of 'Epic'. Up until 1993, there had only been a small handful of songs recorded which contained such a style, so when the likes of Biohazard and Onyx teamed up, as well as Helmet and House of Pain, Slayer and Ice-T, and Faith No More and Boo-Yaa T.R.I.B.E., *Judgement Night* became the first full-length rock and hip-hop album to ever be released.

Faith had been approached to contribute to various movie soundtracks around this time and *Judgement Night* appealed to the band the most. Reaching out to Boo-Yaa T.R.I.B.E., an American Samoan group who incorporated funk and metal elements into their spicy dose of gangsta rap, the two bands came together to write and record 'Another Body Murdered'. A powerful and bruising song in which Boo-Yaa supplied the rap vocal leads, Roddy Bottum's piano riffs and keyboards brought some Faith No More familiarity, as did Mike Patton when his harsh screams reinforced a rousing chorus. A crunching instrumental came from Billy Gould playing the guitar in Jim Martin's absence, which in turn allowed Boo-Yaa to take on the bass work; and Mike Bordin's raw and uncompromising drum patterns completed the puzzle on this rap rock classic, and one of the finest duets on the whole of the *Judgement Night* soundtrack album.

A music video filmed with Marcus Raboy, who had already created a name for himself in the early 1990s by directing promos for Mary J. Blige, Ice Cube, and Run-D.M.C., featured dark and effective performance shots of both bands playing together, nicely interacting with sequences taken from the movie the song was promoting. Released as the soundtrack's third single, 'Another Body Murdered' reached 26 in the UK, thus helping to bring rap rock further into the public eye. Within a few years, the combination of styles would be one of the biggest sub-genres in music when the nu metal movement rose to mainstream prominence. Limp Bizkit, Papa Roach, and Incubus would be just a handful of bands who would cite *Judgement Night* as one of their biggest influences.

Upon the video's completion, Bordin, Gould, and Patton had finally decided that Bottum's excessive drug use had to be nipped in the bud, and so the trio staged an intervention. Bottum entered himself straight into rehab, where he would eventually be able to overcome his demons and get clean, through an abundance of strength and perseverance.

For Jim Martin, though, there would be no second chance and by November, the band's patience with him had finally grown too thin. Failing to answer phone calls or return messages, the stresses and strains which had begun with his father's passing and became further exaggerated by a lack of interest in the material that was being written for *Angel Dust*; Martin could not be reached when his bandmates demanded to find a solution to their problems. Understandably feeling some sort of pressure in following up *The Real Thing*, *Angel Dust* may have been the polar opposite to its predecessor, and Gould and Patton would openly talk of creating songs to distance themselves from being lumbered with the 'Funk Metal' tag, but in Martin's mind *Angel Dust* was too contrived, and as the months passed and his unhappiness continued to bring the rest of the side down, Faith No More were stuck with the same unsavoury dynamic which had ultimately led to Chuck Mosley's firing. With continued silence from Martin, the quartet had no other choice but to fire him via fax, the method unprofessional but preferable in this instance to avoid any slanging matches or physical interaction. Perhaps they thought Martin would act shocked, but surely even he couldn't have been too surprised when he read his last rites. A talented guitarist, without doubt, the rest of Faith were extremely thankful for Martin's contributions over the years, becoming a key part in bringing the band's true sound to fruition. The true sound Martin felt had been found on *The Real Thing* was that which ultimately proved to be his downfall, and when he wasn't given the chance to replicate those stylings on the next album, it was seemingly downhill from there. On 30 November, the official announcement of Martin's departure was sent out to the world, and with it came the end of Faith No More's activities for 1993.

1994: All Change

The first half of 1994 was largely made up of writing a new album and searching for a new guitar player. A shortlist including Godflesh's Justin Broadrick and Killing Joke's Kevin 'Geordie' Walker at least saw the latter of the two fly out to America and rehearse with his potential new employers, but when nothing came of it, Trey Spruance was waiting in the wings to fill the hole left by Jim Martin's departure.

Co-founder of Mr. Bungle along with Mike Patton, Spruance was more than your average guitarist, his playing and composition style influenced by multiple genres that included folk rock, ska, jazz, and death metal. He was also a more than adequate user of vintage electronic organs and analogue synthesisers, something which would come in handy as the next album's recording process got under way. Asked to add guitar parts to drum and bass guitar demos given to him during his try-out, Faith knew they had the right man when Spruance showed he could base his ideas around keyboard entries, much akin to how the band had always worked with leaving the guitars until last. Being a fan of Faith No More, first and foremost, Spruance also knew what worked and what didn't when writing to suit the band's multi-faceted musical compass.

Instead of receiving a proper contract, the new guitarist was offered a salary deal and, while he had musical talent in abundance, Spruance was less savvy on the business side of being part of a major label band, even though Mr. Bungle were considered major label, of course. Faith No More was a different kind of monster, though. Unfortunately for him, his eagerness to be part of one of his favourite bands was less reliant on money (as it should be), but he would come to find out pretty quickly how little his new gig was really worth financially. Patton appeared the least excited to see his old friend join the ranks, telling Spruance it wasn't an 'ideal situation' and clearly having reservations about broadening their working relationship outside of Mr. Bungle. Spruance was officially announced as Faith No More's new guitarist in July during a feature interview with *Kerrang!* magazine. In a bizarre admission during a 2015 interview with *Metal Hammer*, Gould talked of the band having an initiation ceremony for their new guitarist: 'We have this ring, like a circle of protection. On a full moon, we made him strip down naked, and we had this circle of candles. This is serious. It happened to Trey. They were crazy times'. Okay then.

Twenty songs were written for *King for a Day... Fool for a Lifetime*, and after the rich and convoluted material found on *Angel Dust*, the once again quintet decided to strip back the experimentation and produce songs of shorter length and with simpler structures. Ditching one Wallace for another, Faith approached the in-demand Andy (in no way related to Matt) to produce and mix the album after the stress and strains of getting *Angel Dust* finished had caused Matt Wallace to become somewhat disillusioned with his profession. In 2015, he revealed how he had to distance himself from Faith No More:

> At the end of *Angel Dust*, because it was such a difficult record to make, there was pretty severe acrimony within the band, certainly between everyone and Jim, and there were some really heated arguments. Roddy was having his own struggles with some addiction issues, we were at a recording studio that really wasn't supportive at all, I had to basically produce, engineer, assistant engineer, and answer the phones, and it was a really stressful record to make. So at the end of it, I took off for a couple of months and said, 'I'm done with this music thing for a while', and at the end of that record, I said to those guys, 'Listen, I think it's time for you to find a new producer, a new guitarist, or both'.

An expert in bringing the guitars to the forefront of a song, Andy Wallace first earned a reputation for himself when he teamed up with Rick Rubin to co-produce the Aerosmith and Run-D.M.C. duet 'Walk This Way', in 1986. In an effortless switch from working exclusively with hip-hop artists to embracing the dark side of heavy metal, Wallace went on to engineer and mix Slayer's classic thrash metal triple-header of albums *Reign in Blood*, *South of Heaven*, and *Seasons in the Abyss*, while also giving Nirvana's *Nevermind* that explosive sound which helped in its march towards legendary album status. Making some of the most aggressive music of the early 1990s, it was for this reason that Faith No More wanted to work with Andy Wallace, and he accepted the job providing the band moved out of their comfort zone of San Francisco and join him at his favoured Bearsville Studios in Upstate New York.

Founded in 1969 by Albert Grossman, who at the time managed Bob Dylan and the folk troupe Peter, Paul and Mary, Studio B was opened first, and then followed the much larger Studio A, complete with 2,400 square foot tracking room and a 35-foot high ceiling. Meat Loaf recorded part of his 40 million-plus selling *Bat Out of Hell* album at Bearsville in 1975, and the Rolling Stones rehearsed there in 1978 as they prepared to embark on a huge US tour. After Studio A was remodelled in 1985 to

Above: Not your average boyband. (*Getty Images*)

Below: The unlikely lads with a point to prove (*Getty Images*)

Left: The album that sent Faith No More global, eventually. (*Slash*)

Right: 'From Out of Nowhere' cover art. (*Slash*)

Left: One of the many cover designs for Faith's breakthrough single. (*Slash*)

Right: 'Power Rap Metal'-according to this enticing advert. (*Slash*)

Left: Pulling in bigger UK audiences in 1990. (*Slash*)

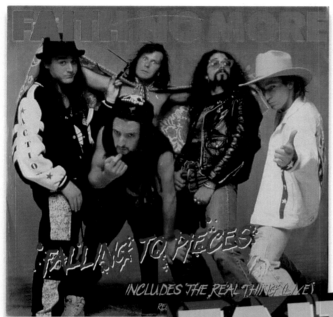

Left: Taking life seriously as usual for the 'Falling to Pieces' cover art. (*Slash*)

Right: Still the band's only official live recording to this day. (*Slash*)

Right: Ready for business down under. (*Slash*)

Left: An advert for Faith's show on 3 October 1991, at the Shibuya Kokaido Hall, Tokyo, Japan. (*Slash*)

PREMIER HARBOUR PRESENTS

FAITH NO MORE

THE REAL THING

AUSTRALIAN TOUR 1990

ITINERARY

ITINERARY

old MMM p1o?
lo4o

FAITH NO MORE

アメリカ西海岸から出現した超過激派バンド、
熱望に応えて追加公演決定！

▽△フェイス・ノー・モア▽

待望の追加公演

10/3 6:30PM
(水)

渋谷公会堂

S=¥5,500 A=¥5,000 (税込)

●主催／ニッポン放送

▶10/2は売切れ

ヘヴィ・メタル、ラップ、ヒップ・ホップ、ファンク、ロック
ン・ロール…様々な要素を混ぜ合わせた先駆的なサウンド
で、一躍シーンに登場した超過激派グループ、フェイス・
ノー・モア。アメリカ西海岸出身の5人組だが、本国はも
とより、イギリスでも圧倒的な人気を得、目下台頭の目と
してぼく進む中だ。いよいよ日本にも一大旋風が起こる。

●お問い合わせ
ウドー音楽事務所
☎03 (3402) 7281

★チケットは8/31(土)より右記にて
前売及びTEL予約開始！

トヨタ 取山チケット・エージェンシー ☎03 (3401) 9999
ウドー横浜 ☎045 (664) 6969
チケット・ぴあ ☎03 (5237) 9999

ANGEL DUST CAN SERIOUSLY
DAMAGE YOUR MENTAL HEALTH

FAITH NO MORE
NEW SINGLE
MIDLIFE CRISIS

Produced by Matt Wallace and Faith

3 Track Coloured Vinyl 7"
3 Track Cassette in Special Crisis' Box which inc
4 Track Picture CD

Coming soon – "ANGEL DUST" – LP ·

On tour with Guns n' Roses in Jun
9 Manchester, Maine Road · 13 Wembley Stadium · 16

Left: The next chapter of FNM kicked off with the brilliant 'Midlife Crisis'. (*Slash*)

Right: When cassettes were still a big thing! (*Slash*)

Right: Mike Patton refusing to bow to *Top of the Pops'* miming convention. (*BBC*)

Left: Who doesn't 'dig' Mike Patton ... A 'Midlife Crisis' video still. (*Slash*)

Right: A video still from the band's best-ever performing single, 'Easy', featuring drag queens and all. (*Slash*)

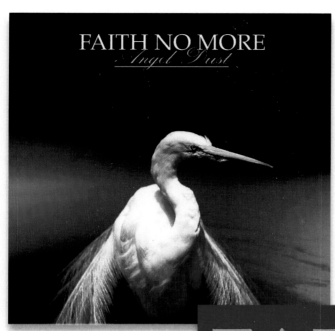

Left: The beautiful *Angel Dust* cover art, with devilish and dystopian music within. (*Slash*)

Right: One of many examples of the classic FNM juxtaposition between song and artwork. (*Slash*)

Above: An eye-catching show poster for the band's 1993 date at the Hollywood Palladium. (*Slash*)

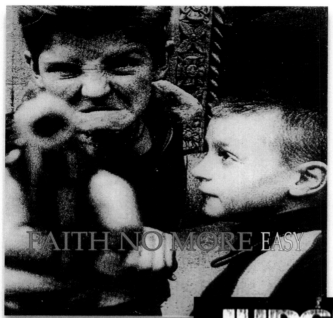

Left: The not-so-easy on-the-eye art for the cover of this Commodores song. (*Slash*)

Right: A decent movie with a ground-breaking accompanying soundtrack. (*Immortal, Epic Soundtrax*)

Right: FNM headlining the Saturday of a stacked 1993 Phoenix Festival. (*Phoenix*)

FAITH
NO MORE
VIDEO CROISSANT

TS

INCLUDES
'A SMALL VICTORY',
'EPIC' & 'WE CARE A LOT'

Left: The band's first music video collection. (*Slash*)

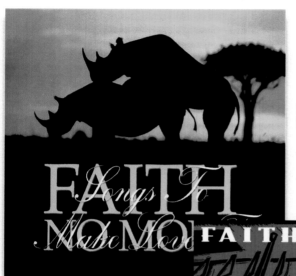

Left: Songs to make (Rhino) love to … (*Slash*)

Right: With a new guitarist in tow, Faith bounced back with *King for a Day… Fool for a Lifetime* in 1995. (*Slash*)

Left: The album's lead single. (*Slash*)

Right: The cover art to the 'Ricochet' single. (*Slash*)

Left: What would turn out to be Faith No More's last album for eighteen years... (*Slash*)

Right: Still able to turn out some excellent tunes, 'Ashes to Ashes' was a pure banger. (*Slash*)

Left: The end was nigh… (*Slash*)

Right: Benny Hill graces the cover for Faith's departing compilation album. (*Slash*)

Left: One more single, oddly chosen by the label to be Faith's Bee Gees cover. (*Slash*)

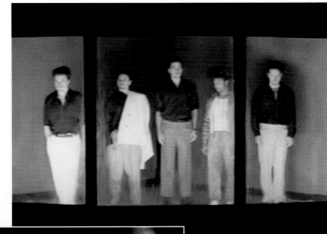

Right: Don't let them near your children… a still from the 'Evidence' video. (*Slash*)

Left: Dean Menta during his brief stint on guitar, starring in the 'Evidence' music video. (*Slash)*

Right: A great shot from the 'Ashes to Ashes' video, signalling the start of the funeral parade. (*Slash*)

SPARKS VS. **FAITH NO MORE**

THIS TOWN
AIN'T BIG
ENOUGH FOR
BOTH OF US

Left: An interesting collaboration, to say the least. (*Oglio*)

Right: A sincerely epic tour line-up; who picked up one of these t-shirts?

GUNS N' ROSES

WASHINGTON DC	MINNEAPOLIS MN
JULY 17	AUG 5
E.RUTHERFORD NJ	MONTREAL PQ
JULY 18	AUG 8
DETROIT MI	TORONTO ON
JULY 21	AUG 9
INDIANPOLIS IN	DENVER CO
JULY 22	AUG 12
BUFFALO NY	SAN DIEGO CA
JULY 25	AUG 14
PITTSBURGH PA	VANCOUVER BC
JULY 26	AUG 17
FOXBORO MA	SEATTLE WA
JULY 31	AUG 18
COLUMBIA SC	PASADENA CA
AUG 2	AUG 22
FAITH NO MORE	FAITH NO MORE

METALLICA

TOUR 92

THEY SAID IT WOULD NEVER HAPPEN

GUNS N' ROSES
METALLICA

WITH SPECIAL GUEST
FAITH NO MORE

Left: Such an incredible line-up, even if the tour would become marred by multiple controversies.

include a Neve 8088 recording console, which had been custom built and previously used by The Who at Ramport Studios in Battersea, London, R.E.M. would be just one of many big-name acts to frequent Bearsville over the next couple of decades, when the Athens, Georgia alt rockers wrote and recorded music for their *Out of Time* and *Automatic for the People* records during their rise to international fame.

Located a couple of miles outside of Woodstock and only 90 minutes from the Bethel dairy farm, which played host to the '3 Days of Peace & Music' festival in 1969, the studios at Bearsville were just one part of a continually expanding plot over the years. Bearsville Records followed in 1970, the label primarily catering for folk and blues rock acts much in keeping with the counterculture generation of that period; and then came Turtle Creek Barn and Apartments, as well as a theatre and a host of restaurants. Pretty much situated in the middle of nowhere, the apartments allowed acts to live on-site for the duration of their recording sessions, and it was a bit of a wake-up call for the members of Faith No More, who were used to the fast-paced city vibes of San Francisco. Gould even likened their stark surroundings in Bearsville to a form of 'sensory deprivation', but at least the band did have some company during their September to late-October stay, when the industrial metal band Fear Factory arrived on site to begin work on their *Demanufacture* album with English producer Colin Richardson.

If the residents of Bearsville wanted to venture further afield and they didn't have their own transportation, only one hire car company catered for the area, and after blowing tyres on three separate occasions, Faith were given a more robust car to travel around in. On the day of getting their upgrade, Patton and Bordin were involved in a scary accident. Clipped by another car, the two Mikes were flipped upside down and sent scurrying down the road before finally coming to a halt. Escaping with only cuts and bruises, the musicians were luckier than the driver of the other vehicle, who suffered serious injuries. According to Bordin, the first the hire company learned of the accident was when their mangled vehicle was returned to them on the back of a tow truck, and even though it wasn't their fault, Faith No More were banned from renting another vehicle for the duration of their stay at Bearsville.

Working as a four-piece for much of *Angel Dust* due to Jim Martin's absence, a similar situation arose for *King for a Day...* when Roddy Bottum sparingly joined his friends in the studio. Still getting over his drug addictions, Bottum's resolve was severely tested when his father passed away in late 1993, and then he lost a close friend, Kurt Cobain, in 1994. The entire rock community was sent into a state of shock upon the news of the Nirvana frontman's suicide by shotgun, announced on 5 April; and having remained close to Courtney Love since her departure from Faith No More in 1984, Bottum was understandably hit harder than most by Cobain's untimely demise.

Unbeknownst to him, until the first day of recording, Trey Spruance was placed in charge of providing string and horn arrangements on some of the songs. Blind scoring and for the most part succeeding with the ideas he came up with, Spruance's input is littered throughout the album. But because of Bottum's minimal involvement – to the point where he only received partial writing credits on two tracks – there is an evident lack of those familiar keyboard elements which had made Faith No More such an unorthodox band in the first place. The recording of *King for a Day...* was completed by the beginning of November, and then Andy Wallace took the album to Soundtrack Studios in New York to mix it throughout the rest of the month.

Faith's next album was in the bag, but their excitement didn't last long when, upon returning home from Bearsville, Spruance threw a spanner in the works by reluctantly quitting the band. Wanting to renegotiate his salary deal and not truly feeling like a full-time member, the guitarist asked to arrange a future date to discuss a new agreement. Met with a lack of assurance as to his position and with management showing little interest in wanting to tie him down for the future, Spruance felt he had no other choice than to walk away. When later discussing his departure, Patton made it clear that he believed the reason Spruance left was because he didn't want to embark on the hectic nine-month touring schedule which had already been arranged to promote *King for a Day...;* and Spruance was quick to shoot down those claims. Remaining professional and choosing to focus on the positives of his time in the band, even after an *NME* article came to his attention which had less than nice things to say about him, Spruance has openly admitted to being proud of the album he helped create, as well as speaking highly of the musical talent that Bordin, Bottum, Gould, and Patton possessed, as well as praising both their characters and personalities.

It had been an interesting year to say the least, and it was a year in which Faith No More played not one single show. The musical landscape continued to change as the decade reached its mid-point, brought on by Nirvana's sad and abrupt ending, which in turn played a big part in the decline of the grunge movement. Something heavier was coming, though, something that would somehow flourish on mainstream radio and TV, and it was rearing its ugly head just a few hundred miles from San Francisco, in both Bakersfield, and Los Angeles. Influenced by Faith No More and fusing together rock music with a hip-hop undercurrent much like 'Epic' had done in 1989, Korn were making early strides in forming the 'Nu Metal' movement; and even on the back of their eponymous debut album released at the end of 1994, no one had so much as an inkling as to what would happen as the new millennium moved ever closer.

With their next album, Faith would quickly find out if they still had a place amongst the higher echelons of rock's elite, but with increasing tension between band members and yet another guitarist in tow, it was impossible to tell what the future held as 1995 began.

1995: King for a Day... Fool for a Lifetime

King for a Day... Fool for a Lifetime

Personnel:
Mike Patton: vocals
Trey Spruance: guitar
Billy Gould: bass guitar
Roddy Bottum: keyboards
Mike Bordin: drums
Record label: Slash, Reprise
Recorded at: Bearsville Studios, Woodstock, New York (September-November 1994)
Produced by: Andy Wallace
Release date: 28 March
Running time: 56:46
Highest chart positions: Australia: 2, UK: 5, US: 31
Tracklisting: 1. 'Get Out' 2. 'Ricochet' 3. 'Evidence' 4. 'The Gentle Art of Making Enemies' 5. 'Star A.D.' 6. 'Cuckoo for Caca' 7. 'Caralho Voador' 8. 'Ugly in the Morning' 9. 'Digging the Grave' 10. 'Take This Bottle' 11. 'King for a Day' 12. 'What a Day' 13. 'The Last to Know' 14. 'Just a Man'.
(All songs written by Faith No More)

By the time of *King for a Day...* we'd had some difficult times, and we knew that if and when we did it, this was gonna be the record of our lives. It had that all-or-nothing feel to us. Instead of putting everything into every song, we wanted to take things out and make them a bit simpler. Perhaps that's what you'd call a 'pop' or lighter feel. All the loud songs turned out really great on this album, really aggressive, and we've always done that really well. But the smoother songs, I've never felt we've gotten exactly right. And this one is pretty damn close to being exactly right.
Mike Bordin, *Metal Hammer*, 1995

Introducing the new album to management and receiving largely positive feedback, there was a sense that after the fallout from Jim Martin's departure and then the coming and quickly going of Trey Spruance, the next era of Faith No More could be the most exciting yet.

It didn't take long to find another new guitarist, in fact, he had been in plain view of the band for years without them even realising it. Assisting

Roddy Bottum as his keyboard tech since 1992, Dean Menta had built a strong rapport with the whole group in the years since, and he also happened to be an able guitar player who had recently produced and performed on alternative metal act DUH's second album, *The Unholy Handjob*, which would also be released in 1995. It was an easy decision to have Menta come onboard, and the door had barely stopped swinging from Spruance's exit when his replacement arrived and immediately set to work on learning Faith's songs for a far-reaching tour schedule that was set to run for much of the year.

The first taste of the *King for a Day... Fool for a Lifetime* album arrived on 28 February when 'Digging the Grave' was released as the lead single. Proving to be another big departure from the previous album, it was during an interview around this time that Mike Bordin revealed how he wanted to emulate the sound of Faith's earlier music, which, in his words, he felt was 'tighter, faster, and harder'. Mission accomplished with 'Digging the Grave' – in and out in just over three minutes and a straight-shooting guitar-orientated rocker. Trey Spruance's mean riffs carried on the heaviness that Jim Martin had once contributed so emphatically, and with the throbbing bass and drum combo creating a tight rhythm section, this was a new Faith No More who no longer relied on Roddy Bottum's keyboards to invoke such a signature sound. It still sounds strange today not to hear Bottum's once essential piece of the band's longstanding puzzle, and with him absent during much of the album's recording, it perhaps demonstrated a hint of a band who, whether consciously or not, appeared to be trying to hold onto the coat-tails of the rock scene in 1995 and not wanting to be left behind. Mike Patton's continually improving vocals contained a selection of joyous cleans and piercing screams, and even as a straightforward rock song, 'Digging the Grave' still contained enough substance in its short running time to rival what most bands were coming out with at the same time.

Impressed by Marcus Raboy's directing skills for the 'Another Body Murdered' music video, Faith brought him back to shoot the promo for the first single. A similarly dark and mysterious video where the band could be witnessed performing in a warehouse space, and also featuring various shots which had been presumably captured around San Francisco and shown at various points, it was certainly one of Faith's more down-to-earth videos in their extensive catalogue; much like the uncomplicated nature of the song, it was supplementing. For one reason or another, though, MTV America barely played the clip and radio completely shunned the song, so it was hardly a surprise when 'Digging the Grave' failed to chart in the US. MTV Europe at least gave it some rotation and it was enough to send the track to 16 in the UK, which in the grand scheme of things could still be deemed an encouraging result. The chart position qualified Faith No More to return to *Top of the Pops* for the first time in almost five years, and it helped that the band was already in the country at the time of recording. Preceding the TV performance, a 'secret' and intimate show at The Old Trout in Windsor welcomed the first Faith No More gig in almost eighteen months while also serving as Dean Menta's debut appearance on guitar. A short tour playing in venues with maximum capacities of around a thousand was in stark contrast to previous visits over the pond, which had taken in much bigger settings. Serving to signal a reset for the quintet, it would become apparent further into 1995 that Faith's popularity was somewhat on the wane if their concert attendances were anything to go by.

The band was back on Channel 4's *The Word* on 3 March, where they performed another new song from their upcoming album, 'What a Day'. Sitting down with the show's host for a short interview afterwards, Billy Gould and Mike Patton were immediately asked about Jim Martin's exit by Terry Christian. Embarrassingly calling the former member Bill and not Jim, Patton's response was to throw a glass of water in Christian's face, and deservedly so, it has to be said. The awkwardness continued with more lazy journalism being met by sarcastic responses, and when Christian introduced Faith's next song, which was supposed to be their cover of 'Easy', the five-piece began playing the early notes of it before instead launching into their rendition of the Bee Gees 'I Started a Joke'. A few days later, Faith were back at Maida Vale Studios to record a special program for Radio 1, with a mini set of 'Digging the Grave', 'I Started a Joke', 'Ricochet', 'Get Out', and 'What a Day'; and on 14 March they were special guests on *MTV Most Wanted*, which also filmed in London. Along with being covered for various magazine features, there was a strong promotional campaign put in place in Europe for *King for a Day...*, suggesting that if the album was going to gain any commercial success, then it was most likely going to occur outside of America. In one particular interview around that time, Billy Gould could not hide his fondness for the album:

The new album was a catharsis for us. We made a record that was very liberating. I think we really learned how to use our power as a unit. I mean, I have a total submarine view of it, but I see it as more of a release-type thing. There is a great amount of stress let off on this album. It's heavier, it's more direct, and it's the first record we had the guitar the way we wanted it. Now it feels like we're a dog who's been let off the leash.

Officially released on 28 March (a limited vinyl pressing had come two weeks earlier), *King for a Day... Fool for a Lifetime* contained the artwork of graphic novel artist and painter Eric Drooker, the images used taken from his American Book Award-winning *Flood! A Novel in Pictures*. Gracing the album's front cover was Drooker's rabid dog and hostile policeman piece, which was one of many prime examples to strongly contribute to the theme of the book, where powerless citizens of New York struggle to deal with authority in a rapidly deteriorating city. The image would become more synonymous with Faith No More than with Drooker, but you can bet a good few people picked up his graphic novel on the back of being introduced to his work through picking up their copies of *King for a Day...*

If fans wondered whether the band's comments on *King for a Day...* being made up of simpler songs was just a ruse, 'Get Out' backs up many of such statements as the album kicks off with a two-minute burst of antagonistic hard rock. Mike Patton's opening line of 'What if there's no more fun to have' appears to find the singer questioning whether his bandmates have much left in the tank, but that was just the beginning of a journey that soon becomes fascinating through its instability. Extremely guitar-driven, Trey Spruance's heavy riffs competed nicely with Mike Bordin's cyclical snare snaps, and the stripped-back production allowed the song to venture into a garage rock setting. 'Get Out' was all of Patton's own making, and although it was far less fractious than his last solo attempt ('Malpractice'), the song ushered in the latest incarnation of Faith No More with no dramatics and with not a keyboard in sight.

Followers of Rage Against the Machine could be forgiven for confusing the opening moments of 'Ricochet' with one of their own tracks, or in particular the groovy guitar as the work of Tom Morello; as Spruance's funk-fuelled lead riff brings to mind the early moments of the rap rock quartet's showcase track, 'Killing in the Name'. But that is where the similarities end as, from then on, 'Ricochet' became a Faith No More classic in the making. Written on the day of Kurt Cobain's suicide, the lyric of 'I'd rather be shot in the face than hear what you're going to say' seems poignant in its coincidence, and after being asked by journalists what inspired the line, with Cobain's death being hinted as a possibility, Mike Patton refused to confirm whether his words were inspired by the Nirvana icon or not. The last song to be completed at Bearsville, 'Ricochet' almost failed to make the cut until it was championed by Bordin. Seeing promise in the sombre verses which built up and formulated into a memorable hook, it is bizarre how after almost being axed from the album, 'Ricochet' would end up being the second single choice. Bordin spoke of his attraction to 'Ricochet' with *Kerrang!* in 1995:

> That's my favourite song. It wasn't going to be on the record, but that song turned out so great that it pushed another song off the record. I really love the choruses, where it gets really big and it really takes off. I love that song. And that was the last song we wrote as well. That was the twentieth song we wrote for the record.

Radiohead and Tool would reference US comedian Bill Hicks in some of their songs over the years and Faith followed suit on 'Ricochet', where Patton included the humorous 'It's always funny until someone gets hurt, and then it's hilarious' line he adopted from a quick-witted Hicks joke which had long been part of his stage routine. Still missing any semblance of Roddy Bottum, 'Ricochet' maintained the early simplicity of the album before things took their first surprising turn as 'Evidence' swooned in next.

Composed of a glorious bout of jazz-influenced R&B, this brilliant little number was built upon by a prominent piano lead, smooth bass, bluesy guitar solos, and Patton's pure singing. Perfectly encapsulating the band's collective and eclectic influences, Patton called 'Evidence' a 'great pop song', believing its results would not have been possible if Jim Martin had still been in the band. The spliced string arrangements created by Spruance and performed live in the studio by a string quartet formed a valuable backdrop, and the suave switch in pace allowed a quick breather before a scathing mood changer barged its way into proceedings.

Spruance's guitars on 'The Gentle Art of Making Enemies' are menacingly metallic, complementing Patton's absolutely bonkers maniacal wails and scorching screams; sounding like a man who is verging on a mental breakdown. Believed to be about prison rape, the stark lines of 'If you don't make a friend now, one might make you', and 'I deserve a reward 'cause I'm the best fuck that you ever had' certainly led towards this theory, creating another night and day contrast of successive songs and the kind which had helped Faith's stock rise throughout the 1990s when you didn't know what the five-piece were going to come up with next. Another song penned by Patton after taking Billy Gould's guitar riffs and arranging the whole thing in one night, the dumbfounding psyche that the frontman has always possessed made 'The Gentle Art of Making Enemies' one of Faith No More's most coarse tracks of all time.

Just a short time from now, a band by the name of System of a Down would rise out of Los Angeles with a similarly violent and often oblique sound unlike anyone else around during the nu metal movement. Having openly admitted over the years to being influenced by Faith No More, 'The Gentle Art of Making Enemies' could possibly be one of the primary songs from which the Armenian/American metallers took their inspiration; their fan favourites of 'Sugar' and 'Chop Suey!' containing bearing clear similarities to this *King for a Day...* highlight.

Returning to the visual way of conceiving music, the hyper jazz delicacy of 'Star A.D.' was dreamed up as 'Las Vegas, ripped vinyl seats, dirty shag carpet, and $1.99 buffets', according to Mike Bordin. Mostly written by Gould, 'Star A.D.' is glitzy and cheesy cabaret which starred a live horn section, the Hammond organ, and more assured crooning from Patton. A line from the 1965 French film *Alphaville*, ('When you die, you'll become something worse than dead, you'll become a legend') is the only dark moment on an otherwise upbeat song that is rich in enthusiasm, its high point coming when Spruance's pure blues guitar solos return for further jolly outings. Most likely a conscious decision throughout the album's tracklisting, an intense and evil song is always waiting to drag things back down into the gutter, and as with the duo 'Evidence' and 'The Gentle Art of Making Enemies', 'Star A.D.' was pursued by the frankly vicious 'Cuckoo for Caca'. The heaviest song on *King for a Day...* and one very much located in the same dark ballpark as much of the *Angel Dust* content, the suppressed guitar tone and thrash-tinged drum sections ran parallel to Mike Patton's indecipherable screams. There was still a place for the Hammond organ to deliver small melodies, but the hardcore pace of 'Cuckoo for Caca', which was written about eating shit (yep!), almost acted as a prelude to a sound that would become commonplace throughout the Noughties with the emergence of metalcore, and the evolution of a new and even more brutal form of grindcore.

'Caralho Voador' became the next obscure entry, a bossa nova song much in the style of 1950s and 1960s samba music. Translated from Portuguese to mean 'Flying Dick', 'Caralho Voador' is apparently a popular form of graffiti in Brazil – the penis with wings attached to it most commonly seen scribbled on public bathroom walls. Patton switches between the foreign language and English as he tells the story of driving down Highway 101 whilst picking his nose. Unhurried and with some gentle percussion and tasteful keys, the song acted as a kind of mid-album break before 'Ugly in the Morning' announced itself with a penetrable bass and drum salvo, swelling key chords, and another abrasive guitar lead. In many ways carrying the flow of Faith No More songs of old, the ambiguous wording and haywire vocal deliveries keep an element of originality that the band had always been able to offer, and the final barrage of cacophonous instrumentation built upon by Patton's latest regurgitating plummet into insanity, only reinforced the frenzied state of both the song and the band during that specific period of the writing and recording sessions.

Following 'Digging the Grave', 'Take This Bottle' carried Faith into country music waters. Described by Roddy Bottum as 'Guns N' Roses music with Hank Williams lyrics', this ballad of sorts proved to be a stunning inclusion where every instrument worked together in perfect timing and structure. The twanging guitars and bass groove in the verses created an ideal setting for some of Patton's most heartfelt words he had ever put to a song, very rarely heard in such a mindset but capable of causing a lump to form in the throat when he tells a presumed loved one to walk away so he can feel the same pain that he has caused to them. On an album where the majority of its songs were more simplistic, there was still plenty of eye-catching songwriting on show and 'Take This Bottle' soon became of the biggest success stories. Choosing to build upon Gould's initial song idea, even after the bassist was left questioning whether it was suitable for the album, *King for a Day...* was all the better for having 'Take This Bottle' amongst its tracklisting; and the same could be said for the acoustically charged title track which continued an impressive creative spurt.

With lyrical content surrounding the grim reality of death, the acoustic guitar brought another first to a Faith No More song, zigzagging with Bottum's piano patch to assume the lead on a wholly sincere and mature number. A pulsating middle section born out of a jam session took 'King for a Day' to a completely new level, substantially developed by the combustible energy of a set of musicians who, in that inspired moment, sounded as cohesive as ever before; a spark having lit the touch paper and signalling a second wind as the latter half of the record increased in forward momentum. Similar to 'Get Out' and 'What a Day', its 116-second running time was all that was needed to make its bold statement, before promptly making its exit. As the verses cruised along with a punchy rhythm section, a swift chorus revealed one of the album's finest hooks, with hazy keys filtering through towards the end while Patton rasps the song's title in a final throe of stubborn defiance.

Roddy Bottum described 'The Last to Know' as 'Pearl Jam on mushrooms', when alluding to its exceedingly grungy feel. Unlike any other Faith song past or present, the track appeared to correspond with what else was happening in 1994 when the song was created, as the Stone Temple Pilots, the Smashing Pumpkins and Pearl Jam were evolving out of the murky grunge scene and becoming bona fide rock superstars of their own making. Spruance brought two strong guitar solos, which were nicely layered over further high-tempo guitar segues, using heavy and fuzzy distortion for better effect, while Mike Bordin's talents were fully on show through a rampant assault which utilised the whole of his drum kit.

'Pure pop indulgence' is the best way to describe 'Just a Man', the final song on *King for a Day...* and propelled by orchestral strings, more blues guitar, and some heavily groovy bass. Another important leftfield swerve which illuminated Mike Patton's singing voice, through which his harmonies and melodies flowed effortlessly. Still able to threaten a hostile takeover, however, Patton cleverly incorporated a brief narration piece which he was able to present in the shape of movie trailer monologue, the short bout of irritability backed up by a tempestuous Billy Gould bass riff. Quickly settling back into its original drive, 'Just a Man' also featured a gospel choir to enhance the feelgood factor of the track, and it was another fine example of Trey Spruance's ability to score on the spot; his efforts here closing *King for a Day...* on a triumphant high.

Faith's European tour came to its climax with four French dates, the last of which was on 6 April, and the six-week stint at least helped *King for a Day...* score some decent sales overseas. Reaching number 5 in the UK, the album also secured Top 10 peaks in Belgium, Germany, the Netherlands and Sweden, amongst others, while in America, it only landed at 31 on the *Billboard* 200. Within a matter of weeks, the album had vanished from the US chart altogether, suffering the same fate as *Angel Dust* did not long after its release. Were the times really changing that much in 1995 – enough to find Faith No More being left behind? Had a large proportion of the band's fan base turned off after the dramatic change in sound between *The Real Thing* and *Angel Dust*?

Or was it that even after a good five years of dipping in and out of the mainstream eye, were people simply still not 'getting' the band's music? There was no doubt that certain portions of Faith's back catalogue contained a wealth of radio friendliness, but many of the songs chosen to promote their associated albums failed to light up the airwaves as they should have, and one of the main reasons for this was of the band's own making – burning bridges as far back as 1992, with a hugely controversial 'performance' at the *97 Rock* appreciation party in Buffalo on 1 October. Faith No More had already played a headline show at the State University in the city that night, and then they were invited to an event at the Uproxx Night Club & Theater which was being hosted by *WGRF-FM/97*. Rich Communications owned all the big radio stations in the area, from Buffalo to New York and even farther. The quintet wanted to hit the road to continue on to the following day's venue, but they were advised that by making an appearance at Uproxx, it would go a long way in securing major radio play for any future releases. When the band arrived, they were met with a scene they had not anticipated, nor were they particularly comfortable with, where strippers walked around serving drinks and a bang average Black Crowes tribute band were providing the live music. Asked if they would consider hitting the stage to play a song, Faith borrowed the cover band's equipment and kicked off with a repetitive guitar riff and some equally repetitive Mike Patton word jumble. Anyone in attendance who may have been hoping to hear a rousing rendition of 'Epic' or 'Midlife Crisis' soon realised their naivety, and when Patton shouted '97 Rock, suck my ass' over and over again, things went downhill extremely quickly. Choosing to expose himself and rub the microphone around his manhood, the dip into depravity continued when Jim Martin used the neck of his borrowed guitar to continue 'pleasuring' Patton; the whole room suddenly baying for Faith No More's blood and then getting it when someone in the crowd launched a beer bottle at Patton's head, the direct impact busting the singer wide open. A second bottle would also hit Patton, but not before he had retaliated against his aggressor by swinging his mic into the face of the attacker and sending him flying to the ground. Making a quick getaway to the sanctuary of their waiting tour bus, Faith got the hell out of Buffalo before the cops arrived, as Patton's antics had ingrained themselves into many of the audience's brains and scarred them for life. The evening's events made front page news on the following day's issue of *USA Today*, as they did in a handful of local publications, and needless to say Faith No More would very rarely, if ever at all, get played on Rich Communications' multitude of radio stations over the coming years.

'You could scratch anything from Detroit to New York City,' said Billy Gould when looking back on that night with slight regret, 'just take that part of the map out. We were done, that was it, goodbye, rest in peace. Never to be played on rock radio again'. At the time, the band didn't care about their exploits, going as far as to say they had a good night and even offering to return another time to repeat the exact same performance – sexual stimulation from a microphone and guitar neck and all.

After promoting *King for a Day... Fool for a Lifetime* in Europe, Faith flew to Australia for an easter weekend festival triple-header, and while over there, they were invited back onto the *Hey Hey It's Saturday* TV show to perform 'Evidence' (Patton sang while the rest of the band had to mime their playing). Throughout much of the decade, the Big Day Out event had been Australia's premier festival, but in 1995, Alternative Nation was set up to offer another option for music fans. Taking place between 13-16 April, the first two dates were held in Brisbane, before singular shows in Sydney and Melbourne quickly followed. The line-up remained the same throughout, headlined by Faith, as well as Lou Reed, Nine Inch Nails, Tool, and Primus. The event could and probably would have been even bigger had the original headlining duo of the Stone Temple Pilots and Red Hot Chili Peppers not pulled out beforehand, and that was likely to be the main reason why ticket sales were less than projected. There were also restrictions on alcohol consumption which certainly didn't go down too well with many of the attendees, and after the 1995 event, Alternative Nation would not be held again.

Continually and unconditionally taking Faith No More to their hearts, *King for a Day...* once again earned its best chart position down under, reaching two on the ARIA listings. The album was only kept off the top spot by Silverchair – Australia's new favourite sons who had released their debut album *Frogstomp* in the same week as Faith's fifth effort. What was even more remarkable was that the trio, who fed off the grunge movement and were trying to keep its sound alive even after its mainstream decline, were all just fifteen years of age when *Frogstomp* was issued to the world.

In 2015, Gould further discussed with *Metal Hammer* his own frustrations with how Faith No More's popularity was especially meandering in the US come 1995, which ultimately led to *King for a Day...* suffering as a consequence:

By that time, we knew our unpopularity in America and our popularity everywhere else was letting us know that we must be doing the right thing because American music was so fucking bad at the time. At that time, we all went off and did solo stuff for a couple of years because we were so tired of all the bullshit that people brought to their experience of Faith No More. But that wasn't fatigue with the music, just with being so fucking misunderstood, which sounds primadonna-ish but it's true. Right now, when people tell me they love that record (King for a Day…), I think, 'Where the fuck were you when it came out then?'

By the end of April, Faith were beginning a five-week US tour with Montana noise punks Steel Pole Bath Tub as support, and having released 'Ricochet' as a single on 1 May, the quintet were guests on the *Late Night with Conan O'Brien* show to further promote the song and its accompanying album. Despite their best efforts, a lack of interest in 'Ricochet' meant it suffered the same fate as 'Digging the Grave' in America and therefore failed to chart. It did get a bit of love in the UK, though, hitting number 27.

A handful of B-sides were also recorded during the *King for a Day…* sessions, four of which were covers equally as diverse as all the previous songs Faith No More had chosen to put their own spin on over the years. 'Digging the Grave' may have been the first track to offer a hint of what was to come on *King for a Day…* but on the CD single release, 'Ugly in the Morning' and 'Cuckoo for Caca' were chosen to act as B-sides. Sandwiched between the two album tracks was 'Absolute Zero', another one written entirely by Mike Patton but chosen not to be included on the record because of the near hour-long running length it had already amassed. Feeding off more metallic guitars and a classic Mike Bordin drum clinic, 'Absolute Zero' was perhaps one heavy song too many to be included, and while it was probably a good decision to relegate it to a B-side, it did make the single a more appealing purchase as, back in 1995, there wasn't really any other way to come across non-album songs. Often imitating the original styles of the songs they chose to cover, 'Greenfields' was given a modern rehash through the use of electric and industrial-sounding drums, and a pensive piano riff. Originally written, recorded, and released in 1969 by Seattle folk group The Brothers Four, 'Greenfields' sold over one million copies and earned a gold certificate back in the day; and Faith No More's prosperous cover, which featured on the CD Maxi version of 'Digging the Grave', found Trey Spruance's guitars sounding like something out of the 1960s. But it was Mike Patton's dulcet tones that really stood out with another masterful singing performance, and it was yet another reminder that no vocal style has ever been beyond his limits.

Precursing 'Greenfields' was the cover of the Bee Gees' 'I Started a Joke', first released by the Gibb brothers in 1968. Faith's take included the smoothest vocal performance you will ever hear from Patton, and at certain moments it even sounds like the vocals are being performed by someone else entirely. Very much a pop song like the original, the acoustic guitar was once again dusted off, but this time it was Dean Menta who contributed to the track, as Trey Spruance had left the band before the cover had been recorded. A warping bass line, layered backing vocals, and a glittering string section made 'I Started a Joke' a cheesy delight for the modern age. Like 'War Pigs' had drawn in a heavy metal following in 1989, had times been the same by 1995, there is no doubt that as with 'Easy' in 1993, 'I Started a Joke' could have enticed a completely different type of audience into checking out Faith No More, and they would have surely found much of their original material to their liking too.

Backing up 'Ricochet' on its single release was a cover of the notorious GG Allin's 'I Wanna Fuck Myself', which found Faith going full-on punk rock. A raucous take as fast and nihilistic as Allin's version, it was imperative the quintet kept some of that classic DIY hardcore essence, as emphasised by Patton's purposely raw and muffled vocals, which paid homage to Allin's ability to build a cult following despite his music being poorly recorded and produced. 'I Wanna Fuck Myself' was also the second of two tracks where the guitars were recorded by Dean Menta, and they were the only song credits he would receive during his time in the band.

There have been multiple versions of 'Spanish Eyes' recorded over the years and Faith's take remains one of the last. The song's first incarnation was an instrumental composed and performed by German bandleader Bert Kaempfert, in 1965 and under the title of 'Moon Over Naples'. A year later, lyrics were added by Eddie Snyder, best known for co-writing 'Strangers in the Night' with Frank Sinatra. On this occasion, Snyder's lyrics went towards swing maestro Al Martino's song, which now went under the title of 'Spanish Eyes', and it would become a big hit in both America and Europe. Further artists to produce their own rendition include Andy Williams, Bing Crosby, Elvis Presley, and of course, Faith No More, who produced a similarly vintage-sounding track with horns and relaxed drumming playing second fiddle to Patton's crooning vocal.

All of the above covers are worthy of their place in the Faith No More vault, but even they couldn't tempt enough people to go out and buy the singles they featured on, so for many a year, they probably went largely undetected by a large proportion of Faith's fanbase until file-sharing and digital streaming allowed easier access to non-album tracks.

Another TV date on 26 May had Faith performing 'Digging the Grave' and 'Evidence' on *The Jon Stewart Show*; the event pre-recorded because on the same night the program aired, the quintet was playing Pointfest 3 at the Riverport Amphitheatre in Maryland Heights, Missouri. An annual show put together by St. Louis radio station KPNT, 1995 would actually host two Pointfest events, but Faith's would only play the first one where they were joined by The Stone Roses, Collective Soul, and Bush. The four bands then moved on to the following day's Q101 Jamboree in Tinley Park, Illinois, where Sheryl Crow, Duran, and KMFDM were also part of an eclectic bill. A day later, Faith was in Somerset, Wisconsin for Edgefest II, headlined by punk rock icons the Ramones.

A summer trip to Europe was mostly made up of festival slots, but there were also a few small headline shows thrown in for good measure, and in July, Faith returned to the UK's Phoenix Festival for another Saturday night headline spot. Part of the heaviest line-up of the three days and also including a lethal dose of hip-hop, Public Enemy, Ice-T and Body Count, Pitchshifter, and Paradise Lost were there to warm up the ever-growing crowd ahead of the main event on the main stage. Performing ten tracks from *King for a Day...*, Faith also made room in their set for some fan favourites, as the five-piece treated a passionate audience to energetic displays of 'Epic', 'We Care a Lot', and 'Midlife Crisis'.

Released in the UK on 17 July (some websites cite 8 May for other parts of the world), 'Evidence' was the third and final single taken from the latest album. Reaching 27 in Australia and 32 in the UK was as good as it got for the sumptuous R&B number. Filmed in a San Francisco nightclub, the Walter Stern-directed music video debuted a new look for the band, who could be seen dressed in suits and ties (Patton didn't have a tie, but he still looked rather dashing). Performing 'Evidence' in an enclosed room, where on the other side of large panes of glass were a relaxed audience sitting at tables and sharing a drink and chat with their chosen company; largely neglecting the band and relegating their display to nothing more than background music, which could easily have been the intention of the video's plot all along.

Unlike the last time Faith No More played Phoenix Festival, their latest visit wasn't to be their final show of the year, as next they moved on to New Zealand, Australia, and Japan, before reacquainting themselves with their Brazilian fanbase on another South American trek. Joining the Monsters of Rock touring festival for consecutive shows in Sao Paolo, Santiago in Chile, and Argentina's capital city, Buenos Aires, Faith No More shared the stage with headlining act Ozzy Osbourne, as well as Alice Cooper, Megadeth, and Scandinavian rap metal mob, Clawfinger. KROQ's Karma Concert at the Concord Pavilion in California on 15 November would round off the band's show schedule for the year, and without knowing it at the time it would be their last until 1997, as a planned six-date UK arena tour which would have been some of Faith's biggest shows in the country was cancelled. Later giving one of the reasons for the cancellation to be because they were set to retreat and work on another new album, it soon became apparent that other commitments had started to become more of a priority for certain band members. On 22 August, Brujeria released their second album, *Raza Odiada (Hate Race)*. Once again featuring Billy Gould under his alter ego, Güero Sin Fe – translated to poignantly mean 'Blond without faith', another album full of brutal death-infused grindcore continued where *Matando Güeros* had left off prior, and this time the content shone a heavy focus on the theme of immigration (not that it was easily understandable being that the songs were sung in Spanish and in a bludgeoning death metal vocal style). Also, in 1995, Mike Patton and Trey Spruance had mended their bridges and were back on the same page for the sophomore Mr. Bungle album *Disco Volante*. The title in reference to the yacht of the same name, which can be seen in the James Bond film *Thunderball*, *Disco Volante* would be Bungle's most experimental album of all as the near 70-minute running time delved into everything from death metal to jazz, easy listening to tango, and it even incorporated a little bit of Arabic music too. Faith No More had been due to visit the UK between 15-25 November, and it is likely more than a few British fans were left feeling aggrieved when they learned of Mr. Bungle kicking off a US tour around the same time – the first show taking place on 18 November at First Avenue in Minneapolis when Faith No More should have been rocking the NEC Arena in Birmingham.

1996: Paths of Glory?

It wasn't a complete fabrication that the November tour of the UK had been knocked on the head so Faith could start work on another album, a sudden burst of creativity taking hold of certain members in order to try and keep the train rolling, even if it hadn't been so long since the release of *King for a Day... Fool for a Lifetime*. As early as January, Billy Gould, Roddy Bottum, and Mike Bordin took charge of the first drafts of some new songs, while Mike Patton continued touring through America and into Europe with Mr. Bungle. Bottum's mind was also becoming increasingly elsewhere, though as he prepared for the release of his other band's album. Calling it a 'release valve' and treating the project equally as important as Faith No More, Bottum had joined forces with Lynn Truell, Will Schwartz, and Jone Stebbins to form Star 69 in 1995; a quirky pop rock troupe who quickly changed their name to Imperial Teen. Coming up with songs which appeared to contain influences of the proto-punk stylings of The Velvet Underground and the alt rock dynamics of The Pixies, Imperial Teen allowed Bottum the platform to fully express both his personal and artistic expressions, the keyboardist-turned-vocalist, lyricist, guitarist, and drummer taking on a more expansive workload for his new project. Basing much of his lyrical content around gender and sexuality, the happy/sad musings and immediate hooks of the songs earned higher praise than Faith No More ever had at times, and with Slash Records fighting their corner, the band's debut album, *Seasick*, arrived to generally positive reviews on 7 May.

Not content with recording Faith and Mr. Bungle albums in 1995, Patton was also putting the finishing touches to his first solo album, but the mindset he was in when recording the 'songs' in various hotel rooms during the *King for a Day...* world tour remains extremely questionable. Made up entirely of vocal sounds Patton had recorded onto a TASCAM four-track Portastudio, *Adult Themes for Voice* consisted of 34 tracks, with many of them ranging between just ten and twenty seconds in length. Belligerent and utterly incomprehensible, the vocal-only composition was so disparate and inaccessible that the album effectively served as one 43-minute piece, and released on 23 April (in 1996) through John Zorn's Tzadik Records, *Adult Themes for Voice* was critically and clinically panned. 'Noise for the sake of noise', and 'Expensive lessons in buyer's remorse' were just two scathing one-liners from various reviews, and quite what Patton was thinking when he decided to do something like this is anyone's guess. Unsurprisingly, the album did not sell well, and anyone who says they listened to it on repeat is almost certain to be lying.

Containing much more substance, Patton had also contributed vocals to a song on *Roots* – the sixth album by Brazilian metal behemoths Sepultura. Veering away from their original death metal style in favour of delving into groove and nu metal territory come 1996, having been empowered by Korn's groundbreaking 1994 debut and ensuring the services of in-demand producer Ross Robinson to emulate the sounds he had captured on the Korn album, the impressive 'Roots Bloody Roots' and 'Ratamahatta' weren't the only imperative listens on *Roots*. Patton's nightmarish input on the crushing 'Lookaway', which also featured further guest spots from Korn's singer Jonathan Davis, and Limp Bizkit turntablist DJ Lethal, led to the album track receiving equally strong plaudits as the aforementioned singles. Also recorded during those album sessions, Patton lent his fraught vocal stylings to 'Mine', where his threatening whispers and venomous passages of screaming psychosis were parlayed by Sepultura's intense strain of meaty Brazilian metal. Not included on *Roots*, 'Mine' was instead included on the 1997 album *Blood-Rooted*, which was made up of unreleased tracks, B-sides, cover songs, and live recordings.

In the early months of the year, Faith No More were once again short of a guitar player, as Dean Menta had become the latest to quit the band. Already suffering from burnout after a full-on touring schedule throughout much of 1995, having never experienced such a severe stint on the road as a professional musician before, Menta was then unable to connect with his bandmates on a creative level. 'I got pushed off the boat before it totally sank', Menta admitted in a later interview, but the all too familiar outcome was that Faith needed another guitar player, and fast. Kyuss had recently lost Josh Homme, the six-stringer deciding to leave the stoner rock group in order to put the wheels in motion for the birth of his next band, Queens of the Stone Age. Invited to try out for Faith No More, Homme accepted and ventured to Frisco to at least have a jam, but it became apparent early on that the formula wasn't right for what Faith wanted to do next. Whether he even wanted the gig or not is unknown, but Homme was unlikely to be too fussed about missing out as, in a few years' time, Queens of the Stone Age would become one of the biggest rock acts on the planet. Who doesn't love singing along to 'Feel Good Hit of the Summer'?

And then Billy Gould called Jon Hudson after the duo first met in 1993 when Gould produced a demo for Hudson's new wave band at the time, Systems Collapse. When looking for Jim Martin's replacement, Hudson had been sent some *King for a Day...* demos and he recorded some of his own ideas by way of an audition, but of course, he missed out to Trey Spruance on that occasion. Upon parting ways with Menta and choosing to pass on Homme, Hudson wasn't to be denied again when, without even having to audition for the position, he was offered the gig and immediately got to work in helping write Faith's sixth album. Twelve songs were initially tracked before they were then shelved, and although the album was half-written and recorded by March, the sporadic involvement of certain band members meant the songwriting process meandered along throughout the spring and summer.

In April, Mike Bordin joined Ozzy Osbourne's band, a dream opportunity for the drummer having first been approached by the 'Prince of Darkness' when catching the Black Sabbath legend's eye during the previous year's Monsters of Rock shows in South America. In late 1995, Osbourne released his first album in over four years (*Ozzmosis*), and when it was time to hit the road to promote it, Bordin replaced Deen Castonovo; his heavy metal influence heard on particular Faith No More songs now finally exposed on a much larger scale, and joining a band made up of like-minded musicians supporting one of the genre's greatest ever frontmen. This didn't mean Bordin had walked away from the band that helped make him, and while out on tour with Ozzy and during his time off, he was still able to contribute to the new album's writing process. Jon Hudson was already settling in nicely and impressing his new friends by bringing big ideas to the table, thus reinforcing Billy Gould's belief that he had finally found the right guitarist and one who wasn't just a good player but also a good thinker and a good writer. All that Faith No More needed now was for Mike Patton to return to action.

Marrying Italian artist Cristina Zuccatosta in 1994, Patton had since moved to Italy and was now residing in Bologna, the largest city and capital of the Emilia-Romagna region of the country. Although trying to split his time between Bologna and San Francisco, on multiple occasions, the singer would fail to show up when previously agreeing to, and this caused a lot of frustration to Gould in particular, who was trying his hardest to get the album finished. In the autumn, all five members finally laid down basic tracks at Brilliant Studios, even though they were never once in the same room together throughout, but after two weeks of tracking, twenty songs were near completion. Opening in 1989 and owned by Norm Kerner, Brilliant Studios was designed and built to Kerner's exact personal specifications. Located in downtown San Francisco, the studios became the West Coast's prime base for 1990s alternative rock, and as there was a five-bedroom apartment also on the site, it meant that artists could live-in while they worked on their music. Kerner became a much-in-demand producer, engineer, and mixer, putting his stamp on multiple albums throughout the decade, including releases from The Breeders, Melvins, and Neurosis. Kerner also composed, produced, and mixed for TV and film, and in 2007 he left Brilliant behind and opened Perfect Sound Studios in the Hollywood Hills on LA, to meet the demands of a new and modern music industry.

Faith No More may have utilised Brilliant Studios to the best of their ability, but Norm Kerner provided little input. The band decided to produce album number six themselves, with Gould taking it upon himself to act as executive knob-twiddler. Accepting valuable input from former Swans percussionist Roli Mosimann, Gould would invite him to his home studio and, joining a common trend as the 1990s progressed, Faith No More were introduced to Pro Tools for the first time. Mosimann taught Gould how to transfer the tracks recorded in analogue at Brilliant into Pro Tools, which took a monotonous 30 hours in total to do, so long in fact that the process was split across two sessions. Mosimann also taught the fledgling musician-come-producer how to digitally edit songs, with which, since its early 1980s inception, Pro Tools had been continually pushing the limits of what was possible with digital audio. In the years since, Pro Tools has become the industry standard Digital Audio Workstation (DAW), and in 1996 Faith had decided to take a leaf out of everyone else's book instead of playing the role of outsiders like they had been doing pretty much ever since their formation.

Just as in 1994, Faith No More didn't play a single live show in 1996, but between Bordin, Bottum, and Patton, the trio amassed plenty of road and air miles throughout the year and more than made up for Faith's lack of stage time. Imperial Teen embarked on a fruitful set of shows across America, Mr. Bungle followed up their US run by visiting various countries in Europe, before moving on to Australia; and Mike Bordin had been through almost every part of America and Canada with Ozzy Osbourne, as well as playing Monsters of Rock at Donington in the UK alongside KISS. Later in the year, the first incarnation of Osbourne's Ozzfest was held over two consecutive days in October. Spread across two stages, a mix of up-and-coming acts were given important exposure on the smaller second stage, while the main stage boasted the headlining

Ozzy and a stacked undercard of metal heavyweights such as Fear Factory, Sepultura, Biohazard, Danzig, and Slayer. In the years that followed, Ozzfest would only become bigger and better, and it would travel all the way across America for weeks on end and then spread across Europe once fully established. As the nu metal movement took shape, Ozzfest would become the most important heavy metal festival on the calendar, and one that every band tried their utmost to be a part of.

1997: Album of the Year

Album of the Year

Personnel:

Mike Patton: vocals

Jon Hudson: guitar

Billy Gould: bass guitar

Roddy Bottum: keyboards

Mike Bordin: drums

Record label: Slash, Reprise

Recorded at: Brilliant Studios, Razor's Edge Recording, San Francisco, California, 1996-January 1997

Produced by: Billy Gould, Roli Mosimann

Release date: 3 June

Running time: 43:04

Highest chart positions: Australia: 1, UK: 7, UK: 41

Tracklisting- 1. 'Collision' 2. 'Stripsearch' 3. 'Last Cup of Sorrow' 4. 'Naked in Front of the Computer' 5. 'Helpless' 6. 'Mouth to Mouth' 7. 'Ashes to Ashes' 8. 'She Loves Me Not' 9. 'Got That Feeling' 10. 'Paths of Glory' 11. 'Home Sick Home' 12. 'Pristina' (All songs written by Faith No More)

This record took a year and a half to make – serious hard work. I mean, the reason I'm the producer is because I've been living with this thing every step of the way. I couldn't rest until this record was finished. Angel Dust was like a hurricane coming – a big, ugly storm. *King for a Day…* was like when the storm was hitting you, with all this stuff flying all over the place. And this record … this is kind of like digging through the wreckage and pulling out bodies afterwards.

Billy Gould, 1997

Bob Biggs loved *The Real Thing* so much that he wanted it to be titled 'Album of the Year', and while Faith shot down his request at the time, who knew that eight years later, they would revive the title for their sixth studio effort. Even back in 1989, it would have been a rather self-indulgent move to call your own record the best release of the year, but it would have actually had an air of justification in this instance, as song after song came packed with multiple delights and memorable hooks, and eventually, *The Real Thing* deservedly earned worldwide acclaim. But things were very different in 1997.

According to Roddy Bottum, the album title was chosen by Billy Gould after he came across an internet sex chatroom of the same name, so perhaps Biggs' initial suggestion had been long forgotten about; but nonetheless, *Album of the Year* was chosen as the name of Faith No More's next effort. Because of the trials and tribulations that went into getting the record finished, the quintet would personally call it their 'Miracle baby', which in itself would have made for a good name, as would 'Epitaph', but more on that shortly.

The first Faith-related release of the year was Mike Patton's second solo album, *Pranzo Oltranzista*, which was obscurely based on the *Futurist Cookbook* by Filippo Tomasso Marinetti – written all the way back in 1932. Patton is a well-known 'foodie' and has openly admitted that, while on tour over the years, he likes to try different cuisines and new dishes, and the songs on his sophomore effort were linked to culinary themes. Performed by a full line-up of musicians which included John Zorn and playing a type of avant-garde jazz, the song titles were all in Italian with certain ones translated to 'Raw Meat Torn by Saxophone Sound', 'Geraniums on a Spit', and 'Explosion in the Throat'.

On 22 April, Faith No More played their first live show in eighteen months and their first with Jon Hudson on guitar, at the London Hippodrome. Recorded for the *BBC Late Show* with Mary-Anne Hobbs, an interview was conducted, and the band performed 'Midlife Crisis', 'The Gentle Art of Making Enemies' (with changes to certain crass lyrics), and the newbies of 'Ashes to Ashes' and 'Last Cup of Sorrow'. Anyone who paid attention to the content of the latter songs may have been able to grasp that all was not well in the Faith camp. The quintet remained in Europe for the next month, playing one-off headline shows in Sweden and the Netherlands, a couple in France, three in Germany, and then UK dates at the Glasgow Barrowlands, Nottingham Rock City, and the London Astoria. The final show saw Mike Patton famously hit his head on Mike Bordin's drum riser during the closing 'Caffeine', causing blood to explicitly pour from the nasty wound. When performing 'Ashes to Ashes' on Channel 4's *TFI Friday* two days later, the aftereffects of Patton's injury remained clearly visible, although masked as best as possible by a few butterfly stitches.

Album of the Year was given a 3 June release date which coincidentally tied in with Faith's fifteen-year anniversary, and two weeks before its unveiling 'Ashes to Ashes' was issued as the first single. As with much of the tracklisting, 'Ashes to Ashes' was melodic, slower, atmospheric even.

This time around, Faith No More had elected to create a compact set of songs which wouldn't deviate too far from one another, containing 'More feelings and more balance', as Patton described it, and 'possibly darker too'. The lead single perfectly emphasised Patton's statement, a hard-rocking anthem which was less reliant on chaos and instead more polished in its delivery whilst still managing to contain the Faith No More blueprint. Opening with a gritty Jon Hudson riff before settling down with Bottum's sauntering keys and one of Patton's most soaring vocal performances of his whole career, even the gloriously catchy chorus gave the positive impression of a band who were coming back from the edge and hitting full form once again. In 2016, Billy Gould looked back on the song with a degree of fondness:

> It's kind of like when you eat something and all the ingredients fit together. You can't really say why you like it, but it's just you know you like it; it has the scope and it has the melody and it has the impact. It gives me all those things I need that make me feel good.

Directed by Tim Royes, the music video presented a suited and booted band playing in a murky and decaying room before they become surrounded from every angle by an audience of waving arms. The fact the quintet looked like they were dressed for a funeral could have been one of the first precursors to Faith's impending expiration.

Reaching 15 in the UK singles chart meant another invitation to *Top of the Tops*, where eagle-eyed fans were quick to notice a different drummer was behind the kit. A week prior, Mike Bordin had joined up with Ozzy Osbourne for a six-week travelling Ozzfest, and so Robin Guy from British rockers Rachel Stamp was asked to fill in. Early on in the performance, Patton can be seen giving Guy the middle finger, as the drummer was supposed to wear a paper mask with Bordin's face on it. Just before the song kicked in, the mask fell from Guy's face and he was unable to gather it in time, leading to Patton's moment of evident annoyance. Elsewhere, 'Ashes to Ashes' made it to 7 in Finland, 8 in Australia (and went gold for 35,000 copies sold), and 23 in America on *Billboard*'s Mainstream Rock chart.

And then came *Album of the Year*, its cover art portraying Tomàš Masaryk – the first president of an independent Czechoslovakia and who would later be considered the country's founding father. Serving in office until the age of 85, Masaryk passed away two years later, in 1937, and in the album's inner art, photos of his funeral are shown alongside his personal motto, which in English meant 'Truth prevails'. Faith felt able to relate to Masaryk, likening their attempts at melding various musical styles to what Masaryk had done in bringing different people and places together and making them one; thus becoming a symbol for democracy in the process, while Faith No More became equally influential in the music world.

Jon Hudson brought the nucleus of 'Collision' to the drawing board, having taken note of previous album openers in order to create a fiery first song very much built on the band's quiet-loud dynamic. With a heavy guitar burst, punchy bass, and a welcome return for Roddy Bottum's tense keys, 'Collision' was a jarring beginning, much in the same way that 'Get Out' had got the ball rolling on *King for a Day... Fool for a Lifetime*. A handful of sounds which resemble the guitar were actually fused by Bottum running keyboard string sounds through a Tech 21 SansAmp, the ugly textures made possible in such a way, while low and harsh waves of synth were added, which almost impersonated Billy Gould's bass. Hudson's early songwriting efforts had already proved fruitful, and he didn't stop there because 'Stripsearch' was also conceived by Faith No More's newest line-up addition, taking the band into trip-hop waters while at the same time solidifying his own position within the ranks. The most atmospheric of all the tracks on *Album of the Year*, the slick and hypnotic slow burner showed the band were still capable of trying something new, the ethereal strings and orchestral synth movements only adding to the song's intrigue.

'Last Cup of Sorrow' offered one of the first hints of the quintet's shaky ground, the prophetic Patton line of 'Everything you know and ever knew will run through your fingers just like sand, enjoy it while you can', indicating the hourglass was beginning to run on empty. Built around a leading Gould bass chug and a simple but groovy guitar riff, Patton's muffled vocals were produced by him singing through a vintage Telefunken tube mic which was then heavily compressed for further effect, and then a strong chorus of reflection provided the highlight on an honest and uncomplicated arena rock anthem. It is in its simplicity that *Album of the Year* thrives the most, but with a fully focused Roddy Bottum back in the fold once more, his use of subtle electronics provided further substance throughout the record, and none the more so than on 'Last Cup of Sorrow'; which from the first listen was an obvious choice for a future single release.

Only Mike Patton and Faith No More could write a song about email, but what is more surprising is that they chose to do it in 1997 when the internet was still in its infancy and a while away from really taking over people's lives. 'Naked in Front of the Computer' was all of Patton's making, receiving sole credit for this two-minute bruising affair much faster in tempo than most of the album, whilst feeding off an ascending and descending guitar riff. In parts punk rock and in other parts hardcore, this raw rocker tells of Patton's then-increasing obsession with how people could communicate and build relationships through a computer, without ever having to physically talk to or meet the person on the other end. 'Until the memory's full, in how many ways, words, can you say nothing', the singer vents with some of his angstiest deliveries on the record; forever able to find influences in the most unusual of settings.

In the same way that *King for a Day…* went back and forth with a heavy track followed by a slower one, *Album of the Year* has similar traits from time to time, as 'Helpless' next emerged in the form of a chilled acoustic number all about feelings of despair. The longest song on the album at almost five-and-a-half minutes, 'Helpless' slightly outstayed its welcome as the lethargic and repetitive tone found Faith No More hitting a brick wall for the first time. Even Patton's whistling during a tentative bridge sounded like he couldn't get into the swing of things, instead begging for the track to come to an end as soon as possible. Thankfully, 'Mouth to Mouth' would get things back on track. Inspired by Gould's trip to Eastern Europe in 1995, it was during a trek through Albania that he came across what he called 'Ottoman-inspired' street music. Wanting to recapture the sound for one of his own songs, Gould bought an Arabic version of a cheap keyboard, and 'Mouth to Mouth' did indeed provide an interesting change of scene as the middle eastern-sounding keyboards brought a touch of classic Faith No More to the modern day. Combining with a metallic bout of instrumentation, the meaningful line of 'I can dress up the dead man, but I can't bring him back to life', once again sounded like Patton was flogging a dead horse, but the song made for a vital inclusion which somewhat ruffled the feathers along the way.

After the lavish 'Ashes to Ashes', the lounge music/R&B ballad of 'She Loves Me Not' showed a band who were trying to write their own soulful pop song, on the back of the success they had unexpectedly achieved with their cover of 'Easy'. Patton's falsetto vocal remained stylishly smooth, bolstered by some extremely delicious melodies. The memorable line of 'I'm right here where you want me to be' appeared to show a lyricist who was finally happy to reveal his softer side, and even though 'She Loves Me Not' talks of unreturned love, perhaps Patton's recent marriage and new life in Italy had seen him sourcing happier lyrical inspirations. Planned to be the album's fourth single but then later scrapped, it is also worth noting that 'She Loves Me Not' has never once been played live.

Another short and sharp stab followed as the overly happy 'Got That Feeling' tells the story of a compulsive gambler. 'Loving every minute of it, got that feeling I can't stop winning' sings a cheeky Patton, who once again received sole credit for the track. Full throttled with frenzied guitar playing and some staccato drumming, the fun and frantic number is soon replaced by 'Paths of Glory'. Presented by a huge wall of sound and relying on rich and dense atmospherics that do not ever become overwhelming, the implementation of shrieking guitar chords and weighty synth help build towards a grand and exhilarating finale. Stanley Kubrick had previously been referenced in Faith's 'Falling to Pieces' video when Patton dressed up as Alex DeLarge from the *A Clockwork Orange* movie, and Kubrick is once again given the nod here as the tenth track on *Album of the Year* took inspiration from the film director's 1957 flick of the same name. *Paths of Glory* would also become one of Kubrick's earliest critical successes.

Not quite hitting the two-minute mark, 'Home Sick Home' leaned on the side of the psychedelic, but it also gave the impression of being an interlude rather than a full song. Made up of minor-key blues riffs, fuzzy bass, and a baritone Patton vocal with quick fluxes of vitriolic screaming here and there, had it been a little longer in length, then 'Home Sick Home' could have grown into one of the better album tracks, but instead, it felt only half-finished and therefore a little lacklustre.

'Pristina' was not the average Faith No More album closer, but it was another inspired by Billy Gould's trip to Europe and, in particular, a visit to the Kosovan capital during the Balkan conflict, which was only two years away from war at that point. As much an epitaph for Faith No More as it was a sombre dedication to the city that the song was named after, 'Pristina' lived off a repeated guitar chord and its elongated feedback. Experimental in sound and with later shifts in both the bass and keyboards, the mood surrounding 'Pristina' felt like Faith saying their final goodbyes while they still had a platform to do so. 'I'll be with you, I'm watching you' sings a slightly emotional Patton during its dramatic conclusion, and in ten or so months' time, it would turn out to be an even more powerful and lasting imprint of the band's final song, on their final album.

Album of the Year reached 41 on the *Billboard* 200 without any prior airplay, but within a few weeks, it had exited the chart. Faring better in Europe as per usual, multiple top five placings weren't quite as impressive as a peak 7 in the UK, while in Australia, the album powered to number 1 and earned platinum certification in the process. Today, *Album of the Year* has only amassed around 300,000 album sales, which is a similar number to *King for a Day...* Knowing where they were most appreciated, Faith's next tour took in many more dates overseas than in America, but before the quintet flew to Europe, they celebrated their nation's independence day by joining Creed, Our Lady Peace, and Mighty Joe Plum for the 7th annual World's Largest Barbecue at Pinella's County Fairgrounds in Tampa, Florida. The following day and just down the road in Sunrise, Faith headlined Zetafest, playing another set that included more than half of the songs found on their latest record.

Four festival appearances in Italy, Switzerland, and Austria had to be cancelled when Mike Bordin returned to San Francisco for the birth of his first daughter, and so the 15 July date at the Spodek Sporthall in Katowice, Poland, kickstarted Faith's latest European exploits. Five days later, they were back in Stratford-upon-Avon for the year's Phoenix Festival, but this time there wasn't a headline slot waiting for the five-piece. Playing on the Sunday was also a first, but in another clear sign of the band's fading demand, they were fourth down the bill and therefore took to the stage in the middle of the afternoon, preceding the Scottish rock group Texas, the electronic duo Orbital, and the main attraction – the iconic chameleon that was David Bowie.

On 5 August, 'Last Cup of Sorrow' was released as *Album of the Year's* second single, and it was accompanied by a rather extravagant music video which parodied the 1958 Alfred Hitchcock film, *Vertigo*. Mike Patton took on the role of Detective John 'Scottie' Ferguson (originally played by James Stewart), who was hot on the trail of Kim Novak's character, Madeleine – on this occasion, played by the flourishing Hollywood starlet, Jennifer Jason Leigh. The Joseph Kahn-directed video recreated some of the movie's most famous scenes, such as the opening rooftop sequence and Madeleine's suicide dive into the San Francisco Bay. Adding in some light-hearted humour, Billy Gould can be seen dressed as a woman at one point, and at the end, when Madeleine escapes a shadowy figure at the top of a bell tower, the stalker is revealed to be Mike Bordin, and he is eating a bagel. 'Last Cup of Sorrow' reached 14 on the Mainstream Rock chart in America, and apart from hitting 15 in the Polish singles chart, the song didn't do anything elsewhere – even being shunned by fans in Australia and the UK.

'Stripsearch' was due to be the third single and Faith even went as far as to film a video with Philipp Stölzl in Berlin. Following a theme based on a screenplay that Billy Gould had written, the video followed Mike Patton as he approaches a military checkpoint, where at the same time, all five band members can be seen on screen and standing in the queue. Looking rather shady, Patton then does a runner as his passport is being checked, and after being caught and arrested at gunpoint, the rest of the short film builds towards revealing Patton as a criminal. Even though CDs were pressed and the song was added to radio playlists, the single release was then cancelled at the last minute.

On 6 October, Jim Martin released his *Milk and Blood* solo album via the German indie label, Steamhammer. A year prior, the guitarist had made his musical return from the doldrums when he played on Voodoocult's self-titled second album. When the band first formed, the German-American outfit were considered a thrash metal supergroup because of the involvement of Death's Chuck Schuldiner, Mille Petrozza from Kreator, and Slayer's Dave Lombardo. By the time a second album was due, none of those three musicians were part of Voodoocult anymore, but Jim Martin was, and the riff machine played an important part in helping create a solid follow-up to its higher acclaimed predecessor.

Martin's solo project first went under the name of The Behemoth, but once he discovered the Polish black metal band Behemoth was making big strides further afield, he resorted to using his own name to release *Milk and Blood* – a groove metal record in which Martin also sang and acted as its producer. He was even able to get Metallica's James Hetfield to provide some backing vocals, as well as having Hetfield's bandmate, Jason Newstead, guest on 'Fatso's World'. The most fascinating moment on the album was the penultimate track, though – a re-recording of 'Surprise! You're Dead!'; however, the poor mixing and the less than inspiring vocals turned the song into a disappointing mess which found Martin seemingly holding on to past glories. Just three years after his acrimonious departure from Faith No More, even Martin's old affiliation with the band didn't account for much when his latest creation faded into obscurity in the blink of an eye.

Back in America for a set of festival and headline club shows through September and into October, Rockstock '97 in Illinois had a strong line-up which, along with Faith No More, offered Joan Jett and the Blackhearts,

Megadeth, Helmet, Seven Mary Three, and Silverchair. Also on the bill was an up-and-coming rap metal band by the name of Limp Bizkit, who were starting to take America by storm on the back of their recently released debut album, *Three Dollar Bill, Y'All$*. Reluctantly, Faith took Limp Bizkit on the road with them for their US run after being told by their management that the only way the tour was going to be supported was if Limp Bizkit were on the bill too.

The nu metal movement was firmly in its swing by the middle of 1997. Korn had a second album to their name by now and were just a year away from becoming one of the biggest mainstream metal bands in history, Coal Chamber and Powerman 5000, both of whom had played the second stage of the very first Ozzfest, had released albums in the first quarter of 1997, and before the year was out, Snot, Incubus, Hed PE, and Deftones would also become major players in the nu metal game. There were rap metal bands, hardcore punk bands, funk metal bands, gothic rock bands, and while many of their sounds were vastly different to one another, what most of them had in common was a love and respect for Faith No More. Citing the quintet as a key influence and openly discussing the theory of how 'Epic' in particular had turned heavy music on its head, it showed that it wasn't necessarily Faith's sound that had endeared them to so many 1990s upstarts, nor had they birthed the nu metal movement (Mike Patton still remarks how much he hates that era of music), but what did put them in that 'Forefather' bracket was their ability to be able to fuse so many different styles into one complete package, whether it be rock and rap, or funk and metal – it was their 'No Rules' outlook which encouraged others to follow in their footsteps.

Limp Bizkit were regularly booed by Faith's fans throughout the tour, which kicked off in St. Louis on 9 September. Even their abrasive cover of George Michael's 'Faith' couldn't win the crowds over. Fronted by a cocky and rightfully confident Fred Durst, the red baseball cap-wearing, expletive-filled whippersnapper pissed off a lot of people during Limp Bizkit's rise to superstardom, and during one particular show on the Faith tour, he responded to the boos by calling the audience 'Faggots'. Apparently unaware of Roddy Bottum's sexual orientation, Durst was sent with his tail between his legs to apologise to Bottum and the rest of Faith No More. Despite the hardships on stage, there was never any personal trouble between the two bands, and it is likely there were at least a few new Limp Bizkit fans made on that tour, whether people dared to admit it or not.

Further highlighting the changing of the heavy metal tide come 1997, Summer Slam (not to be confused with the annual *WWE* wrestling event) at the Sandstone Amphitheatre in Bonner Springs, Kansas, on 26 September, saw Faith and Pantera babysitting Limp Bizkit, Coal Chamber, and the thrash-turned-rap-metal quartet, Machine Head; while on 4 October in Tempe, Arizona, a young band by the name of Grey Daze joined the Faith tour for a one-off date where they acted as local support. The significance of this mention is that the band was fronted by an unknown Chester Bennington, who in just three years' time would become the lead singer of Linkin Park, a rap rock ensemble who would go on to sell a staggering 100 million-plus records worldwide.

Adding new covers to their sets, Faith took on Aqua's party pop song 'Barbie Girl', R. Kelly's vomitathon, 'I Believe I Can Fly', Deep Purple's 'Highway Star', and Will Smith's 'Men in Black', as the tour rolled over to Australia, New Zealand, and Japan. By mid-November, the five-piece were back in Europe and performing in Croatia and Luxembourg for the very first time, before a week-long UK run included another pitstop on the *TFI Friday* show to once again play 'Ashes to Ashes'. On 6 December, Faith joined punk rock kings Bad Religion in Innsbruck, Austria, for the Quiksilver Air & Style event, where both bands performed while wearing thick-set clothing because of the ice-cold weather. It was a snowboarding event, after all. Faith's final show of the year came a day later, at L'Aeronef in Lille, France.

Somehow, Faith still had time to contribute to another album in 1997. Art pop darlings, Sparks, decided that for their seventeenth album, poignantly titled *Plagiarism*, they would include new takes on some of their most popular songs. When you think of Sparks, the song that instantly comes to mind for most of us would be 'This Town Ain't Big Enough for the Both of Us', and who better to pimp the track up to then-modern-day standards than Faith No More. Mike Patton effortlessly duetted with Russell Mael and the instrumentation was given a heavier and contemporary update, and also featuring on *Plagiarism* was the Faith-featured 'Something for the Girl with Everything', which was another melodramatic bout of cheesy rock. Also credited on the album was Dean Menta, who would then become a full-time member of Sparks in time for their 2002 album, *Lil' Beethoven*.

Only two B-sides have ever been shared with fans from the *Album of the Year* sessions (there are supposedly at least eight other recorded songs that have never seen the light of day). Added to Japanese editions of the record and also backing up 'Ashes to Ashes' on its single release, 'Light Up and Let Go' and 'The Big Kahuna' are both combative rock tracks, the first of which could have easily fitted onto the original album tracklisting. With shorter verses to let the catchy hook excel, it is easily the pick of the two songs, however 'The Big Kahuna' does have a certain charm to it, especially during its fascinatingly eerie middle section displaying a deep bass tone, warping electronics, and dizzying echo effects. Two strong B-sides and the only ones considered good enough to release in some way, the question remains; what else did Faith No More record during the *Album of the Year* sessions, and why have they never let us hear them?

1998: Last Cup of Sorrow

Although the live shows on the *Album of the Year* tour went without a hitch, behind-the-scenes, Faith No More was just about on its last legs. As 1997 was drawing to a close, the group met to discuss what came next, having already received plenty of show offers for the first half of 1998. Three April dates would see Faith grab some sunrays at the Esparrago Rock Festival in Grenada, Spain, on the fourth, headlining day one over Ocean Colour Scene, Chumbawamba, and a host of national acts. Faith would then move on to Porto and Lisbon in Portugal, but any other business which needed attending to at was left up in the air for the time being.

Still taking in a rather outsider's view, Jon Hudson could see the band he had only been a part of for a matter of months was fading fast. Billy Gould was mentally and physically drained from making *Album of the Year*, almost single-handedly keeping the project alive while others dragged their heels and contributed if and when they could; and for the first time, even Gould had lost his motivation in keeping things pushing forward. Hudson loved being in the band and his journey was still in its infancy, but the guitarist had no other alternative than to enjoy the ride the best he could and for as long as it lasted; and as rumours of Faith's disbandment began to increasingly circulate online, the reports actually appeared to carry some validity to them as it became evident that the end of Faith No More really was nigh. In 2015, Hudson spoke to the band's official fan page, *Faith No More Followers*, remembering back to having the feeling that *Album of the Year* was going to be the quintet's final work:

> I viewed everything as an opportunity. I could see the pressure of trying to deliver another great record was wearing on some of the guys because they were putting their energies into other areas or projects. I felt like this might be their last record, so I wanted to make sure I enjoyed it as much as I could.

The trio of European shows were successfully completed, and then the band were offered the opportunity to co-headline a European tour with Aerosmith. By doing the tour, Faith would earn a potential payday of around half a million dollars, which was easily the biggest sum of money of their career, and it was surely a tour that was impossible to turn down. Aerosmith had been riding a second wave of mass popularity after their well-received 1986 collaboration with hip-hip pioneers Run-DMC had set the hard rockers up for a huge next decade made up of mega-selling albums and sold-out arena tours. Releasing their second number 1 album in a row in March 1997, the multi-platinum *Nine Lives* would be toured around the world for well over two years, and the second European leg in which Faith No More had been invited to join was scheduled to begin in Saint Petersburg, Russia, on 26 June.

The core quartet of Faith called a meeting to discuss whether they should take the tour or not, but it didn't take long to work out that no amount of money on the table was going to stop the ship from sinking. At the time, Roddy Bottum was well on his way to completing work on Imperial Teen's sophomore album, and Mike Patton was already investing in another new project – a metal supergroup which also featured Dave Lombardo from Slayer, Buzz Osborne from the Melvins, and Patton s long-time bandmate in Mr. Bungle, Trevor Dunn. Fantômas had even plotted their first live show to take place in June, around the same time that the Aerosmith tour was due to kick off. Ultimately, though, it was Mike Bordin who was the first to bow out when he was required to join back up with Ozzy Osbourne for the 1998 edition of Ozzfest. Once Bordin confirmed his intentions of choosing Ozzfest over the Aerosmith tour, the death knell for Faith No More had begun to sound. The day after the band members went their separate ways, Patton announced Fantômas debut show at Slims in San Francisco, and as various music news outlets put two and two together and began reporting of Faith's demise, Gould felt an official statement needed to be made. Quickly preparing a short but blunt piece which was released to the media, Gould wrote:

> After fifteen long and fruitful years, Faith No More have decided to put an end to speculation regarding their imminent breakup... by breaking up. The decision among members is mutual, and there will be no pointing of fingers, no naming of names, other than stating, for the record, that 'Puffy' (Mike Bordin's nickname) started it. Furthermore, the split will now enable each member to pursue his individual projects unhindered. Lastly, and most importantly, the band would like to thank all of those fans and associates that have stuck with and supported the band throughout its history.

It was slightly sardonic that Faith No More would gain greater coverage over their split than they had for the last five or six years for their musical output, and in a further twist of irony, the Aerosmith tour, which effectively led to Faith No More calling their own bluff, was cancelled after Steven Tyler suffered a cruciate knee ligament injury during their late-April show in Anchorage, Alaska.

Bordin, Bottum, and Patton dealt with the split by burying their heads into Ozzfest, Imperial Teen, and Fantômas, respectively, while Jon Hudson hid his own disappointment by working on some new music of his own. Patton could have been even busier from 1998 onwards if his claims of being asked to sing for INXS are to be believed. When Michael Hutchence was found dead in a Sydney hotel room on 22 November 1997, the globally popular Aussie pop rockers had an important decision to make: should they fold and leave behind a legacy built upon by the multi-platinum success stories of their *Listen Like Thieves*, *Kick*, and *X* albums; or continue on with a new singer – someone with the vocal dexterity required to take INXS further while also paying homage to the man who had helped the band become one of the biggest of the last two decades. Supposedly asked to keep their advances secret after he had mockingly turned down the gig, but not before suggesting performing with the band with a noose around his neck (Hutchence's death had been ruled a suicide by hanging), Patton revealed these details during an interview on Australian radio. Continually pressed to discuss the INXS offer, Patton finally flipped his lid and revealed the noose comment, its timing less than ideal as the interview had gone out during National Suicide Awareness Week and was also heard by Hutchence's parents, who were listening to the broadcast. Patton has showed brief hints of remorse since that interview, but he has never hidden how much he dislikes INXS' music. Speaking to the East Bay Express in 2002, he called the band 'Fucking godawful', and 'Dingo-loving sons of bitches'.

In 1995, Patton enlisted John Zorn, Trey Spruance, Chris Cochrane, and Bill Winant for another noise rock and jazz fusion project under the moniker Weird Little Boy. Also incorporating some dark ambience into another haywire jaunt which one review described as 'A brutal noise experience for listeners interested in how far sonic technology can really be stretched and twisted', the one and only album stemming from the collaboration promoted the musician's collective influences in an unabridged and befuddling manner. Released via the Japanese label Avant on 12 April 1998 – some two-and-a-half years after being recorded, *Weird Little Boy* was a largely forgettable entry in the Mike Patton cannon, but the ideas behind the project were best illustrated on the three-part eleven-minute opener, 'Two Weeks on a Morphine Drip/New Dirt and New Flies/

Lorne Greene', full of ear-splitting noise, belligerent sound effects, and saxophone entries thrown in to really send the listener into oblivion.

Cashing in on Faith No More while they were still fresh in people's memories, Slash Records released a compilation album on 24 November titled *Who Cares a Lot?* The only involvement from any of the band members came from Gould, who had been hit the hardest by the split and wasn't able to bury himself into something else so quickly. Suggesting the album should act as a greatest hits collection, *Who Cares a Lot?* was made up of all the single releases which were placed in chronological order for the tracklisting. The compilation, therefore, opened up with the 1987 version of 'We Care a Lot' and closed with 'Stripsearch'. An interesting inclusion was track twelve, the cover of 'I Started a Joke' originally by the Bee Gees, which would be given a single release some three years after first appearing as a B-side on the 'Digging the Grave' promo. A music video was filmed for the song, directed by Vito Rocco and set in an English club where an evening of karaoke is taking place. Of course, Faith had been no more for five months by this point, and so none of the band are featured in the video. Instead, British actor David Hoyle takes to the stage to mime Mike Patton's sumptuous vocals. Billed as Faith's final single, 'I Started a Joke' failed to chart anywhere.

The most enticing aspect of *Who Cares a Lot?* was its second disc which was made up of unreleased material, B-sides, demos, and live tracks. Recording during the *Angel Dust* sessions, 'The World Is Yours' was quickly demoted because of the number of samples used in it (even the band gave it the working title of 'Sample Song'). At almost six minutes long, the sounds of a military exercise, an elephant trumpeting, a trance skit, and even an audio cut of Bud Dwyer's public suicide can be heard at certain times, along with an eerie rhythm section which remained on the experimental and darker side of many of the tracks that had made up *Angel Dust*. Patton's cerebral vocals adhered to the menacing vibe, but because of the severe overdose of samples, 'The World Is Yours' was destined to be nothing more than a B-side at best.

In a playful mood during the *King for a Day...* era, 'Hippie Jam Song' found Faith No More recording a song capable of rivalling the alt rock bands of the mid-1990s. A tremendously funky number could have been a slightly tongue-in-cheek jibe at the Red Hot Chili Peppers, containing heavily distorted blues riffs (presumably played by Trey Spruance) and catchy piano chords, even Patton sounded like he was having fun with his happy and vibrant vocal deliveries. The simply titled 'Instrumental' was very much the result of a jam session where Roddy Bottum contributed all the guitar work. Relatively simple and certainly overlong at five minutes, the repetitive nature of the main riff section failed to progress into something more, but 'I Won't Forget You' on the other hand, also a *King for a Day...* outcast, was the most welcome addition on the disc. Gould's spiralling bass line opened an angsty and grunge-tinged number, unlike any other Faith No More song. 'You never love someone, only what they leave behind', sang an unusually sincere Patton, over a feast of churning guitars and energetic drum sections.

Also on the second disc were live covers of Deep Purple's 'Highway Star', and 'This Guy's in Love with You' (written by Burt Bacharach and Hal David), but it was the never-before-heard cuts which really tempted fans into picking up a copy of the compilation. Regardless, *Who Cares a Lot?*, of which the most widespread release featured English comedian and actor Benny Hill, on the cover art, failed to chart in either the US or UK, but it did get to number four in Australia and went platinum for hitting over 70,000 copies sold. Reminding people of just how good a band Faith No More was with a selection of songs that perfectly encapsulated the diversity of their music, even though the compilation wasn't necessarily authorised by the quintet, it still served as a fitting tribute and a slightly a teary-eyed goodbye for some.

A video edition was released in February 1999 under the same name, but the running order was mixed up and started off with the weaker and low-budgeted presentations. 'Ricochet' was omitted from the collection completely for some reason, but there was a place for the lesser seen 'Surprise! You're Dead!' video, which had been made up of footage captured by Billy Gould on a handheld camcorder during Faith's European and American tours in 1989 and 1990. Also featuring behind-the-scenes footage and interviews, there were also performances of 'Caffeine' from a *Hangin' with MTV* episode, and an *MTV Europe* recording of 'This Guy's in Love with You'. Owners of the Video Croissant VHS tape will no doubt have picked up this one, too, to complement their collections.

What Happened Next (1999-2008)

Of all the band members, it wasn't a surprise that Mike Patton was the most productive of the Faith No More five once they went their separate ways. Following the self-titled debut, Fantômas album in April 1999, Patton and Mr. Bungle were set to release their third long-player, *California*, on 8 June. Around the same time, Red Hot Chili Peppers singer, Anthony Kiedis, decided to reignite his rift with Patton, at a time where funnily enough, the two artists were labelmates as both the Chilis and Bungle were signed to Warner Bros. Records.

In a further twist of soap opera proportions, both bands were set to release their new albums on the very same day, and so it was *California* versus *Californication* – the latter chosen as the title of the Chilis' seventh studio effort. It was no secret that Kiedis' troupe were the bigger band and by a considerable margin, and *Californication* was always going to sell in its droves; so it didn't really make sense that Warner would decide to put back the release of Mr. Bungle's album for a further six weeks. To rub salt in Patton's wounds, his band was then removed from selected European festivals, which also featured the Red Hot Chili Peppers on the same bill, at the behest of Kiedis.

Patton bided his time in retaliating, and when Mr. Bungle toured the US later in the year, the band's Halloween show was coincidentally taking place in Kiedis' home state of Michigan, at Clutch Cargo's in the town of Pontiac. The whole band dressed up as their new rivals for the show, with Patton imitating Kiedis by wearing a blonde wig and speaking with a lisp. Even covering some of the Chili Peppers' biggest hits during the set, Patton deliberately changed parts of the lyrics on 'Around the World', 'Give It Away', 'Scar Tissue', and in particular 'Under the Bridge' – where Patton referenced Kiedis' past drug addictions by singing 'Sometimes I feel like a fucking junkie'. The rest of the band also joined in mocking their counterparts, becoming increasingly distasteful when Trevor Dunn approached Trey Spruance, who was dressed as the ghost of deceased RHCP guitarist Hillel Slovak and simulated injecting heroin into Spruance's arm (Slovak had died from a heroin overdose in 1988).

Due to perform at the Big Day Out festival in Australia in the early weeks of 2000, Mr. Bungle were once again booted from the bill at the demand of Kiedis, and with the delay of the release of *California* on top of multiple shows being missed, Patton and especially Dunn would later admit that their band's future had been severely derailed by the Kiedis spat. When the album finally got its release on 13 July, *California* failed to chart and sales were low, while *Californication* became the Red Hot Chili Peppers' most commercially successful record, selling over fifteen million copies worldwide. That would have surely made Anthony Kiedis feel a whole lot better, having got more than one over on Mike Patton.

After finishing the latest Mr. Bungle album and tour cycle, Patton then split his time between Fantômas and another new supergroup, forming the alternative metal Tomahawk with members of Melvins, Helmet, and The Jesus Lizard. Over the next eight years, four Fantômas and three Tomahawk albums were written, recorded and released, but perhaps the most fascinating collaboration Patton would take part in was with mathcore pioneers, the Dillinger Escape Plan. Having lost their original singer and until they could find a full-time replacement, Patton was asked to fill in, the savage and schizo side of his vocals more than suitable for Dillinger's heavy and complex music, which sported fluctuating rhythms, exhaustive tempo changes, and irregular time signatures. A four-track EP titled *Irony Is a Dead Scene* was recorded with Patton. However, by the time it was released in 2004, Greg Puciato had been fronting Dillinger for over a year. Very much a cult favourite within the band's discography, Patton's work on *Irony Is a Dead Scene* was vital in helping the Dillinger Escape Plan's evolution, and throughout the next fifteen years, they would become one of the most popular metal bands around as they continued to pioneer mathcore with sonic experimentation and ear-splitting heaviness.

Mr. Bungle officially called it quits in 2004 after a long period of inactivity, and then Patton made his acting debut a year later, alongside Karen Black, and the duo would play two major roles each in the Steve Balderson-directed thriller, *Firecracker*. Interestingly, Dennis Hopper was due to play the lead in the film, but he was cut from the project and Patton was elevated up from the original plan of having just a small cameo appearance. The singer turned actor would even get into composing soundtrack scores, first for the short film *A Perfect Place* in 2008 and then for Jason Statham's adrenaline thrill ride of *Crank: High Voltage* the following year.

Billy Gould's participation in Brujeria continued when the band released a third album in 2000 titled *Brujerizmo*, which moved further away from the deathgrind stylings of previous efforts in favour of a groove-orientated metal direction; the refined sound more encompassing of the quality ensemble of musicians who were part of the venture. Gould also featured on Fear Factory's 2005 album, *Transgression*, where he laid down some crunching bass on two successive industrial ravaged rippers, 'Echo of My Scream' and 'Supernova'.

After Faith No More had gone their separate ways, Gould teamed up with Mike Bordin and Jon Hudson to work on some new music under the name of Castro Sinatra. Very little is known as to what direction the songs were going in, but after eighteen months of putting an album's worth of material together, the whole project was scrapped when the musicians, and Gould in particular, felt the songs weren't good enough for people to hear.

Roddy Bottum continued on with Imperial Teen, who released two more albums in 2002 and 2007 (*On* and *The Hair the TV the Baby and the Band*), and Mike Bordin's star rose ever higher both on the stage with Ozzy Osbourne, and in the studio. Making his debut on record with Osbourne for the 2001 album *Down to Earth*, Bordin was also part of the band that re-recorded Ozzy's classic solo albums *Blizzard of Ozz* and *Diary of a Madman*, both of which emerged in 2002. Bordin's last release with the Prince of Darkness came in 2007, providing riveting drum sections on the critically acclaimed *Black Rain* record. In 2002, the drummer was also brought into Jerry Cantrell's band in time to record for the guitarist's second effort, *Degradation Trip*, which boasted over an hour's worth of doom-laden heavy metal. The album would be released just two months after the passing of Cantrell's Alice in Chains bandmate and brother, Layne Staley.

At least the quintet had remained busy with being part of various bands in one way or another, but Faith No More's devout fanbase wanted one particular band and one band only ...

The Reunion

There had only been a handful of brief meetings between Bordin, Bottum, Gould and Patton in the years since the split, some even just from bumping into each other in the street, and the distinct lack of communication revealed a sad stagnation of friendships long burned. It wasn't so long ago that the four men were touring the world together, and even though their fanbase had evidently decreased towards the end of the 1990s, there were still many men, women, and teenagers, many of whom had followed Faith No More's career through thick and thin. There were even newer fans who had never witnessed an active band before, as with the new millennium came easier access to music both legally and illegally; and soon, *The Real Thing*, *Angel Dust*, *King for a Day… Fool for a Lifetime,* and *Album of the Year* didn't have to be played on a record player or CD Walkman, the songs could be downloaded on a computer, transferred to mp3 players, or streamed through mobile phones.

Throughout the early Noughties, the band received offers to reform and hit the road. Of all the members, Mike Patton was the one who most frequently and most vehemently shot down any discussion of a reunion, his heavy workload being used as an excuse in him not wanting to take on anything else. Towards the end of 2008, Billy Gould was approached by Warren Entner with another offer, and around the same time, rumours had begun circulating online regarding UK venues being scouted to host Faith No More's return shows. To discuss the rumours and where they may have come from, Gould and Patton met up over coffee and had their first proper conversation in a long time, and it wasn't long after that the duo, along with Bordin and Bottum, were in Los Angeles with Entner to talk about the possibility of getting the band back together. Within minutes of reacquainting themselves, it was clear there was still a chemistry between them, the kind they had fed off throughout the 1990s. It may not have been exactly the same, perhaps a chemistry made up from battle-worn scars which came with airing on the side of caution, but old friends revisited they definitely were. A band of brothers whose love for making music had forged a bond which may have sent them crashing to the ground in the end, but the only slightly broken pieces were able to be salvaged and put back together; not necessarily back to how things were before, but with time comes healing, wisdom, and a will to want to give something another shot. By the end of their gathering in LA, it was decided that Faith No More were coming back.

Music websites continued to report on the reformation rumours, and on 24 February 2009, an official announcement confirmed what many had been praying for but maybe never really thought would happen. Choosing to honour their European following who had helped deliver the band's biggest successes, Faith locked down multiple summer festival appearances across the continent, as well as headline shows here and there. Their first show on American soul would not come until some fourteen months after they had first confirmed their return.

With personal differences set aside, the one big question remaining was whether the reunion would feature the original *Real Thing* and *Angel Dust* era line-up, which of course, meant reaching out to Jim Martin. It had been sixteen long years since the guitarist's firing by fax machine, and with the occasional music release scattered throughout the 1990s and Noughties, Martin's priority switched to pumpkin growing. Becoming a champion in 2005 when his 1,087-pound pumpkin won first prize in a contest just an hour up the road from his Castro Valley home, Martin also competed in other competitions, including the biggest pumpkin festival in the world (Half Moon Bay), and it seemed he had left his guitar-playing days behind him.

Unsure if Martin still held any contempt towards his former bandmates, Roddy Bottum reached out and offered Martin the chance to come back into the fold. Appearing up for the challenge, there was something in the delivery of Martin's words that didn't sit well with the rest of the band, his blasé responses keeping his cards firmly to his chest and only extended upon when demanding a contract be sent to him to make sure the deal suited. The quartet already back in play felt uneasy about partnering up with Martin again, and so they turned to Jon Hudson, who was more than deserving of another opportunity after his first stint came to an abrupt halt.

The biggest date of Faith's reunion tour was their 12 June headline slot at the Download festival at Donington Park in the UK. Headhunted by the festival's booker, Andy Copping, the show would also earn the quintet one of their biggest ever paydays. Download is still one of the biggest rock festivals on the calendar today, and it was far too dangerous for Faith No More's first live performance in over a decade to take place on such a grand stage. Rehearsals went well, but nothing could beat playing in front of a live crowd, and so the band decided to return to the Brixton Academy two days before Download, to blow away any prospective cobwebs and stage rust. Opening the show with a cover of Peaches & Herb's 1978 song 'Reunited' could not have been more appropriate, as its chorus of

'Reunited, and it feels so good, reunited, 'cause we understood, there's one perfect fit and sugar, this one is it' attests to. Faith's performance came across as if they hadn't taken a day off in years, the cohesiveness of all five members enough to confirm they were still up to the task. The Brixton show may have been considered a warm-up, but it still a momentous occasion, and the quintet could not have picked a bigger or more symbolic venue to house their return – such is the history they share with the place. Five thousand lucky spectators were able to have their 'Remember where you were' moment that night, and over 40,000 people had theirs two days later when Faith No More took to the massive main stage of Download to close out the first day of the three-day extravaganza.

A predominantly heavy metal festival which first started out as Monsters of Rock, the first incarnation of Download took place in 2003 as a two-day event. At that time, illegal downloading had reduced the music industry to its knees, causing record labels to lose millions of dollars in record sales, and the artists were at risk of losing their deals in the process. Rock music was arguably the biggest victim of file-sharing, and so Download was a rather apt if not tongue-in-cheek name for a festival that in modern times required the internet to connect prospective audiences and provide frequent information to those who would be attending the year's event.

Over the years, an array of artists from all sub-genres of rock and heavy metal have headlined Download, from nu metal acts such as Linkin Park, Slipknot, and System of a Down, to alternative rock bands like My Chemical Romance, Muse, and Biffy Clyro; and then legendary acts who could still draw huge crowds decades into their careers – Metallica, Iron Maiden, KISS, and Black Sabbath. Faith No More were not out of place on a Download bill, and on the day of their performance, they shared the stage with their old tour buddies Limp Bizkit, who themselves were making their own grand return after a period of inactivity; as well as Korn, and modern screamers Killswitch Engage, Billy Talent, and The Blackout. Headlining the slightly smaller second stage but still bringing in swathes of attendees were Mötley Crüe, the 1980s hair metal heroes also recently returning with their original line-up, and had Andy Copping not spent so much time and money in luring Faith No More to Download, the Crüe could have easily taken the main stage headline slot.

But this was Faith's time, opening their set with the same Peaches & Herb cover as they had in Brixton before ramping up the guitar power with 'The Real Thing' and 'From Out of Nowhere'. From there, the party was well and truly in full flow. Mike Patton may not have had the same youthful energy as he once did, but he was still able to stalk the stage like a kid in a toy shop, his deeper vocals now more fitting for a metal band but still giving a masterclass in strength, depth, and range. 'How's it going Download, are you down, are you loaded?' asked Patton before the start of 'Caffeine', and then admitting his joke was terrible and stale. In the build-up to 'Surprise! You're Dead!', the singer attempted to throw his engaged audience by hinting that the next song was going to be an '80s ballad, but as soon as Jon Hudson came in with that meaty opening guitar riff, everyone knew there was to be no love in the air.

A 23-song setlist was worthy of the admission fee and then some, taking a breather with the likes of 'Easy' and 'Take This Bottle' and then upping the ante with 'The Gentle Art of Making Enemies', 'Malpractice', and 'Cuckoo for Caca'. Patton even incorporated a section of Lady Gaga's 'Poker Face' into the intro of 'Chinese Arithmetic', and by the time the quintet brought the evening to a close with a pulsating rendition of 'We Care a Lot', Faith No More had made the main stage of Download their very own.

In the week leading up to the grand return, a two-disc compilation had been released by Rhino Records to remind people, if there was any need, who Faith No More were. Titled *The Very Best Definitive Ultimate Greatest Hits Collection*, the first disc was made up of two songs from *Introduce Yourself*, three from *The Real Thing*, seven from *Angel Dust*, and three each from *King for a Day... Fool for a Lifetime* and *Album of the Year*. Disc two was full of B-sides, once again bringing 'Absolute Zero', 'The Big Kahuna', 'Light Up and Let Go', 'I Won't Forget You', and 'The World Is Yours' to people's attention in case they had missed them previously. 'New Improved Song' was also included, which of course became 'The Morning After', after the original was heavily reworked.

The focus on the band during their second foray seemed to be far more extensive than ever before, or at least since the era of *The Real Thing*, and for the next few years, Faith No More would continue touring the world when it best suited them, often taking a break after a two or three-week stint, so they didn't burn themselves out. The band members may not have been spring chickens anymore, but they could still go and they could still put many of their younger counterparts to shame with their professionalism and musicianship.

During the third of three consecutive shows at The Warfield in San Francisco on 14 April 2010, Chuck Mosley joined Faith on stage for the first time in over twenty years, where he sung 'As the Worm Turns', 'Death

March', 'We Care a Lot', and 'Mark Bowen'. Mending broken bridges, it was nice to see the former frontman back with his brothers in arms once more, and for a fitting encore, Mike Patton joined Mosley for a duet on 'Introduce Yourself'.

On 2 June 2016, it was announced that a deluxe reissue of *We Care a Lot* would be released after Billy Gould had unearthed the master reels from the original recordings. Getting together once again with Matt Wallace, the two remastered and remixed the tracks that were over 30 years old, and because the band was back on good terms with Mosley, to further honour, *We Care a Lot* Faith No More decided to perform two full shows with their original singer in August, at the Great American Music Hall in San Francisco, and The Troubadour in Los Angeles. Also including 'The Crab Song', 'Spirit', 'Anne's Song', and the title track from *Introduce Yourself*, only 'Jim' was omitted from the debut album in the setlists on both evenings, perhaps the main reason being because Jim Martin was not part of the latest reunion (Jon Hudson remained on guitar). As of this book going to press, and partly because of the global pandemic, which began in the early months of 2020, those two shows remain the last that Faith No More have performed to date.

On 9 November 2017, Mosley would sadly pass away from a suspected heroin overdose, but the part he played in continuing Faith No More's progression will never be forgotten and his infectious personality and raw vocal styles forever remain an integral part of the band's history. Rest in Peace, Chuck.

As the reunion showed no signs of subsiding, the band's creative itch also returned, and they set to work on some new music in 2013. During their appearance at the British Summertime Festival in London's Hyde Park on 4 July, in which Faith were supporting Black Sabbath, they debuted two new songs, 'Superhero' and 'Motherfucker', the latter of which was then released as a 7" single on 28 November to tie in with Record Store Day. On the same day, the five-piece played a surprise mini gig at Amoeba Records in San Francisco.

On 13 May 2014, Faith No More released their first album of new material in almost seventeen years. *Sol Invictus* was distributed by Patton's Ipecac Recordings and put out on the band's own Reclamation Recordings imprint, the album containing a typically diverse set of songs which nicely slotted into the quintet's expansive discography. Running for an economical 39 minutes and without the need to overcompensate in proving a new album was necessary in order to cement Faith No More's reformation, the light-hearted lounge swagger of the title track and 'Sunny Side Up' were neatly pitted against the scathingly brilliant 'Superhero'; its lead riff and keyboard coda alone justifying *Sol Invictus'* existence. 'Cone of Shame' and 'Separation Anxiety' welcomed back Faith's metal edge, and throughout the ten tracks, the keyboard entries from Roddy Bottum galvanised a modern Faith No More on songs they sounded like they were having a lot of fun making. In their review of *Sol Invictus, Rolling Stone* magazine called it 'As much a triumphant victory lap as it is a comeback album', and it is hard to disagree with that statement. Debuting at 2 in Australia, 6 in the UK, and a decent 15 on the *Billboard* 200, the simple and sombre but equally spiteful and brash set of songs earned *Sol Invictus* the Best Album of the Year award at Metal Hammer's Golden Gods ceremony, in June 2015.

A Selection of Setlists

If you have ever witnessed a Faith No More live show, then you will know just how good the band are on whatever stage they take to. Even in the late 1980s, when the quintet was still getting to grips with having Mike Patton as their new singer, their performances were raw and chaotic, but they were also energetic and utterly absorbing. With age may have come maturity and belated sincerity, but even today, Faith No More can still match the intensity of up-and-coming bands, and it will more than likely remain that way until the band finally hang up their boots once and for all. Here are a handful of the quintet's setlists which cover each album cycle, as well as some of their biggest festival slots from over the years.

28 April 1990, Brixton Academy, London
From Out of Nowhere
Falling to Pieces
Introduce Yourself
The Real Thing
Underwater Love
As the Worm Turns
The Crab Song
Edge of the World
The Morning After
Chinese Arithmetic
We Care a Lot
Surprise! You're Dead!
Epic
Woodpecker from Mars
Zombie Eaters
Why Do You Bother?
War Pigs
Easy

10 October 1992, Roseland Ballroom, New York City
Caffeine
Death March
Land of Sunshine
The Crab Song
Midlife Crisis

As the Worm Turns
Chinese Arithmetic
RV
Surprise! You're Dead!
Be Aggressive
Introduce Yourself
Easy
Crack Hitler
We Care a Lot
Jizzlobber
Woodpecker from Mars
Epic
Let's Lynch the Landlord
The Real Thing
A Small Victory

17 July 1993, Phoenix Festival, Stratford-upon-Avon, UK

Caffeine
Be Aggressive
As the Worm Turns
The Crab Song
Midlife Crisis
RV
Land of Sunshine
We Care a Lot
Chinese Arithmetic
A Small Victory
Edge of the World
Falling to Pieces
Surprise! You're Dead!
Woodpecker from Mars
Jizzlobber
Zombie Eaters
Let's Lynch the Landlord
Easy
Introduce Yourself
Mark Bowen
Epic

16 April 1995, Alternative Nation, Olympic Park, Melbourne, Australia

Digging the Grave
Be Aggressive
Midlife Crisis
The Real Thing
Land of Sunshine
Evidence
What a Day
We Care a Lot
Easy
Introduce Yourself
Get Out
King for a Day
Epic
Ricochet
The Gentle Art of Making Enemies
Take This Bottle

6 September 1997, Rockstock, New World Music Theatre, Tinley Park, Illinois

Collision
Midlife Crisis
The Gentle Art of Making Enemies
Last Cup of Sorrow
Evidence
Easy
Introduce Yourself
Got That Feeling
Ashes to Ashes
Home Sick Home
King for a Day
Epic
Naked in Front of the Computer
Just a Man

7 April 1998, Coliseu dos Recreios, Lisbon, Portugal (Faith's final show before their split)

Midnight Cowboy
Collision
Midlife Crisis
Naked in Front of the Computer
Ashes to Ashes
Evidence
Easy
Introduce Yourself
Ice Baby (Vanilla Ice cover)
Land of Sunshine
King for a Day
We Care a Lot
Epic
Just a Man
This Guy's in Love with You (Burt Bacharach cover)
Get Out
Stripsearch
Highway Star (Deep Purple cover)
As the Worm Turns

12 June 2009, Download Festival, Donington Park, Donington, UK

Reunited (Peaches & Herb cover)
The Real Thing
From Out of Nowhere
Land of Sunshine
Caffeine
Evidence
Chinese Arithmetic
Surprise! You're Dead!
Easy
Last Cup of Sorrow
Midlife Crisis
Introduce Yourself
The Gentle Art of Making Enemies
Take This Bottle
Ashes to Ashes
Malpractice
Cuckoo for Caca

Be Aggressive
Epic
Mark Bowen
Chariots of Fire (Vangelis cover)
Stripsearch
We Care a Lot

Full Discography

Studio Albums
We Care a Lot (1985, Mordam)
Introduce Yourself (1987, Slash)
The Real Thing (1989, Slash/Reprise)
Angel Dust (1992, Slash/Reprise)
King for a Day...Fool for a Lifetime (1995, Slash/Reprise)
Album of the Year (1997, Slash/Reprise)
Sol Invictus (2015, Reclamation)

Live Albums
Live at the Brixton Academy (1991, Slash)

Compilation Albums
Who Cares a Lot? (1998, Slash/London/Reprise)
This Is It: The Best of Faith No More (2003, Rhino/WEA)
Epic and Other Hits (2005, Warner Bros.)
The Platinum Collection (2006, Warner Bros.)
The Works (2008, Rhino)
The Very Best Definitive Ultimate Greatest Hits Collection (2009, Rhino)
Midlife Crisis: The Very Best of Faith No More (2010, Music Club Deluxe)

Video Albums
You Fat Bastards: Live at the Brixton Academy (1990, Slash)
Video Croissant (1993, Slash/Warner Bros.)
Who Cares a Lot: Greatest Videos (1999, Slash/Reprise/Rhino)

Single Releases
Quiet in Heaven b/w Song of Liberty (1983)
As Faith No Man, 2-track cassette tape
Chinese Arithmetic (1987)
Promo Only
Anne's Song (1988)
International Issue B-side- 'Greed'
We Care a Lot (1987)
 International Issue B-sides: 'Spirit', 'Chinese Arithmetic (Radio Mix)'
From Out of Nowhere (1989)
European Issue B-sides: 'The Cowboy Song', 'The Grade'. Australian

Issue B-sides: 'Edge of the World', 'From Out of Nowhere" (live Brixton Academy). 1990 European Reissue B-sides: 'Woodpecker from Mars' (live Norwich UEA), 'The Real Thing' (live Norwich UEA), 'Epic' (live Norwich UEA)

Epic (1989)

UK/International Issue B-sides: 'War Pigs' (live Brixton Academy), 'Surprise! You're Dead!' (live Sheffield Octagon), 'Chinese Arithmetic' (live Sheffield Octagon), 'Epic' (live Japanese Bonus Track). Australian Issue B-sides: 'The Morning After', 'We Care a Lot' (live Brixton Academy), US Issue B-side: 'Edge of the World', 1990 UK/International Reissue B-sides: 'Falling to Pieces' (live Brixton Academy), 'Epic' (live Brixton Academy), 'As the Worm Turns' (live Brixton Academy).

Falling to Pieces (1990)

Disc One B-sides: 'We Care a Lot' (live Brixton Academy), 'Underwater Love' (live Brixton Academy), 'From Out of Nowhere' (live Brixton Academy), isc Two B-sides: 'Zombie Eaters', 'The Real Thing' (live Wireless Festival 1990)

Surprise! You're Dead! (1990)

Promo Only

Edge of the World (1990)

Promo Only

Midlife Crisis (1992)

International Issue B-sides: 'Jizzlobber', 'Crack Hitler', 'Midnight Cowboy', Australian Issue B-sides: 'Jizzlobber', 'As the Worm Turns' (Re-recording with Patton vocals)

A Small Victory (1992)

International Issue B-sides: 'A Small Victory (video edit)', 'A Small Victory (album version)', 'Let's Lynch the Landlord', 'Malpractice'. Remix Issue: 'A Small Victory (album version)', 'A Small Victory (R-evolution 23 Full Moon Mix)', 'Malpractice', 'A Small Victory (Sundown Mix)', 'A Small Victory (Sundown Instrumental)', 'A Small Victory (R-evolution 23 Edit)'

Everything's Ruined (1992) – UK Issue Part 1 B-sides: 'Edge of the World' (extended live mix), 'RV' (live Dekalb), UK Issue Part 2 B-sides: 'Midlife Crisis' (live Dekalb), 'Land of Sunshine' (live Dekalb), European Issue B-sides: 'Easy' (Live Munich), 'RV' (live Dekalb)

Easy (1993)

Songs to Make Love To US Issue: 'Easy', 'Das Schutzenfest', 'Midnight Cowboy', 'Let's Lynch the Landlord'. International Double A-side- 'I'm Easy', 'Be Aggressive', 'A Small Victory' (live Munich), 'We Care a Lot' (live

Munich), 'Mark Bowen' (live Munich). Japanese Issue: 'Easy', 'Easy' (live Munich), 'Be Aggressive' (live Munich), 'Land of Sunshine' (live Dekalb), 'RV' (live Dekalb), 'Kindergarten' (live Munich), 'A Small Victory' (live Munich)

Digging the Grave (1995)

CD Single Issue B-sides: 'Ugly in the Morning', 'Absolute Zero', 'Cuckoo for Caca'. CD Maxi Single B-sides: 'Ugly in the Morning', 'Absolute Zero', 'I Started a Joke', 'Greenfields'

Ricochet (1995)

CD Single Issue B-sides: 'I Wanna Fuck Myself', 'Spanish Eyes', CD Maxi Single B-sides: 'Midlife Crisis' (live London Forum), 'Epic' (live London Forum), 'We Care a Lot' (live London Forum)

Evidence (1995)

International Issue B-sides: 'King for a Day', 'I Wanna Fuck Myself', 'Spanish Eyes'

Ashes to Ashes (1997)

Gold on Maroon Cover B-sides: 'The Big Kahuna', 'Mouth to Mouth', 'Ashes to Ashes (Hardknox Alternative Mix)', Maroon on Gold Cover B-sides: 'Light Up and Let Go', 'Collision', 'Ashes to Ashes (Automatic 5 Dub)'. Gold on Black Cover Reissue B-sides: 'Ashes to Ashes (Dillinja Remix)', 'The Gentle Art of Making Enemies', 'Ashes to Ashes' (live) Black on Gold Cover Reissue B-sides: 'Last Cup of Sorrow (Rammstein Mix)', 'Last Cup of Sorrow (Sharam vs Faith No More Club Mix)', 'The Gentle Art of Making Enemies' (live)

Last Cup of Sorrow (1997)

Blue Vertigo Cover B-sides: 'Pristina' (Billy Gould Edit), 'Last Cup of Sorrow (Roli Mosimann Mix)', 'Ashes to Ashes (Dillinja Mix)'. Orange Vertigo Cover B-sides: 'Last Cup of Sorrow (Bonehead Mix)', 'She Loves Me Not (Spinna Main Mix)', 'She Loves Me Not (Spinna Crazy Mix)'. Japanese Issue B-sides: 'Pristina (Billy Gould Mix)', 'Last Cup of Sorrow (Roli Mosimann Mix)', 'Ashes to Ashes (Dillinja Mix)', 'Last Cup of Sorrow (Bonehead Mix)', 'She Loves Me Not (Spinna Main Mix)', 'She Loves Me Not (Spinna Crazy Mix)'

Stripsearch (1997)

Standard Issue B-sides: 'Collision' (live Rotterdam), 'The Gentle Art of Making Enemies' (live Rotterdam), 'Ashes to Ashes' (live Phoenix Festival 1997)

I Started a Joke (1998)

Disc One B-sides: 'The World Is Yours', 'Midnight Cowboy' (live Sydney)

Disc Two B-sides: 'This Guy's in Love with You' (live Sydney), 'We Care a Lot' (live Sydney)
Motherfucker (2014)
Promo Only
Superhero (2015)
Promo Only
Cone of Shame (2016)
Promo Only

Band Member History (In Chronological Order)

Mike Morris: Lead Vocals/Lead Guitar/Rhythm Guitar (1979-1983)
Wade Worthington: Keyboards/Backing Vocals (1979-1983)
Billy Gould: Bass Guitar/Lead Guitar/Backing Vocals (1981-Present)
Mike Bordin: Drums/Percussion/Backing Vocals (1981-Present)
Roddy Bottum: Keyboards/Piano/Rhythm Guitar/Backing Vocals (1983-Present)
Mark Bowen: Lead Guitar (1983-1984)
Courtney Love: Lead Vocals (1983-1984)
Jim Martin: Lead Guitar/Backing Vocals (1983-1993)
Chuck Mosley: Lead Vocals (1984-1988)
Mike Patton: Lead Vocals (1988-Present)
Trey Spruance: Lead Guitar/Backing Vocals/Arrangements (1993-1994)
Dean Menta: Lead Guitar (1995-1996)
Jon Hudson: Lead Guitar/Backing Vocals (1996-Present)

DECADES | Faith No More in the 90s

Faith No More Followers

Almost three-quarters of the world's population has access to the internet, and in this day and age, there isn't much you cannot do so long as you have a computer or a smartphone. For music lovers, the internet has long been a valuable source for providing everything we need to able to stay up to date with our favourite artist's progress, whether it be searching for the latest news, buying concert tickets, picking up some fancy merchandise; or using one of the many streaming platforms to access millions of songs and albums on tap with just one press of a button, for just a small monthly fee.

Online communities allow us to meet new and like-minded people who we can talk to from opposite sides of the world about music, amongst other things, becoming friends through shared interests. If you thought Mike Patton's lyrics on 'Naked in Front of the Computer' were contemptuous enough in 1997, God knows what he thinks about the internet today.

There are plenty of fan sites floating around online, in fact, there probably aren't too many artists who don't have one set up in some form and run by adoring fans who continually offer their unconditional support. KISS has the KISS Asylum, Metallica has the Metallica Club, Tool has the Tool Army; and Faith No More has Faith No More Followers. A non-profit encyclopaedia of all things Faith, both the band as a whole and as separate musicians, what is extra special about Faith No More Followers is that it has the blessing of both the group and their management.

Since its inception in 2014, set up by British superfan Jim Brown, the website and all its accompanying social media pages has only expanded in internet traffic, page 'likes', and mass interaction. Even Mike Bordin, Roddy Bottum, Billy Gould, Jon Hudson, and Jim Martin have been known to give their time and support by being interviewed and also embarking on Q&A sessions with the FNMF community.

The site contains countless press articles dating back to 1988 (who remembers *Melody Maker* and *Sounds* magazines?), the news section is kept firmly up to date, and there are also plenty of fascinating features written by contributors from around the world, celebrating Faith No More's songs, albums, live shows, and any other landmark of interest. Extensively researched, expertly written, and professionally delivered, there is also a heavy emphasis on anniversary pieces when a particular release or a moment in the band's history is about to have its birthday.

100% Faith No More approved, Faith No More Followers does a stellar job in helping keep the band's legend alive and kicking, and if you prefer listening instead of reading, the related *Podcast Croissant* offers regular two or three-hour episodes to cover all bases.

Jim Brown discusses how his love of Faith No More began and how Faith No More Followers came to life:

One fateful day, my big brother came home from school and threw a cassette copy of *The Real Thing* at me, stating 'This is the kind of crap you listen to'. Upon hearing 'From Out of Nowhere', I was immediately rocked to my very core, and suddenly Aerosmith ballads were boring and Alice Cooper looked like a clown. None of my friends had heard of Faith No More so this band was all mine, my thing, my contribution to our collective musical education. I was the kid who loved Faith No More.

Two years later and I had become a true Mike Patton fanboy, with my hair long on top and shaved underneath, wearing waistcoats, baseball trainers, and shorts. Then, along came *Angel Dust* and my childhood fascination matured into an adolescent way of life. That record became my bible, and it influenced every part of my existence. Faith No More ruled every aspect of my life- from my degree studies in art to girls I dated and married, even my future careers. The music shaped my personality.

When the band returned in 2009, I paid three times the ticket value to be at the Brixton Academy for their first show in eleven years. I joined every online forum and fan group there was and soon, I became heavily involved in various sites by sharing my extensive press clipping collection, which I had kept safe for all those years.

In 2012, I joined the team at one of the most active fan clubs and I befriended Bill Gould, which led to me hanging out with the band at Hyde Park in 2014. Noticing that Faith No More didn't have the fan club they deserved, myself and two other Faith-crazed friends from different corners of the globe started Faith No More Followers, the most comprehensive fan group yet. We have interviewed Bill, Roddy, Mike Bordin, Jon Hudson, Trey Spruance, and others affiliated to the band. Working alongside Faith No More has been a dream come true.

From The Author

I'm not ashamed to admit that I grew up as nu metal kid (I can imagine Mike Patton rolling his eyes if he was to read this). During the peak period of that era, between 2000-2003, I would be watching the *Kerrang!* music channel for hours on end and there would be the latest videos from Korn, Limp Bizkit, Linkin Park, Slipknot... the list could go on, but I won't bore you with it. If you know, you know. Every so often, older videos would be sandwiched in between those artists already mentioned, because back then you could phone in and vote for what would come next, and I remember hearing that monumental intro of 'Epic', that heavy bass line, the heavy lead guitar riff, the atmospheric keys; and then that strange rap vocal from a seemingly immature and colourful lead singer. Just one listen was enough for me to want to hear what else Faith No More had in their locker.

If someone was to ask me what my top five albums of all time are, I'm sure a couple of entries would change from day to day, but I know *The Real Thing* is in there somewhere, probably in my top three. I can't think of any other album I have ever played more than Faith No More's third effort, which even today has a timeless veracity to it. *The Real Thing* was the record the band had been threatening since their formation, it just took them a while to make it and it took Mike Patton coming into the fold to finally realise that their lifelong and weighty ambitions could now be made a reality. From the emphatic opening of 'From Out of Nowhere' to the influential 'Epic', to the absolute genius structures of 'Zombie Eaters' and the eargasmic title track; *The Real Thing* demonstrated the collective vision of a band who was built from individual influences, and when the band was one, they invented magic. It's even fair to say that in 1989, Faith No More were well ahead of the curve.

With the emergence of Patton came a new type of lyrical content, where words and sentences were full of opaque ambiguity. There were some songs which he or other members of the band would open up on and divulge the meanings behind them, but many more have been left open to interpretation. If Patton had his way, I think every song in the band's back catalogue would have been left for us to decipher ourselves, especially after what he said during an interview in 1992:

> I don't think we have an obligation to clarify ourselves through our lyrics or even take a standpoint. All five of us simply couldn't agree on any standpoint. If one of us gets a little too outspoken, he's probably lynched

by the others. About the lyrics, it's almost a pity they're printed on the sleeve because the public expects a revelation, that the lyrics will say something about our past, our lives. And to make that kind of connection via some lyric is almost dangerous.

As perfectly proven by the divisive but enthralling *Angel Dust*, the band didn't cater for others, they simply did what they wanted to do and made the music they felt like making. No other artist, past nor present, could ever have come up with the kind of material found on *Angel Dust*, and no one else would have dared risk their career to follow a mainstream hit record with something that was the polar opposite on every imaginable level.

I believe Faith No More never received the credit they fully deserved, and it was slightly ironic that it took them splitting up for some to realise they should have appreciated the quintet while they were around in the first place. Going full throttle (most of the time) throughout the 1990s, the music they made has at least today seen them regarded as rock legends, which is better late than never. But that is the beauty of music – it remains, it is timeless, and it is there when we want to take a trip down memory lane.

Amongst their stunning discography, there is 'Chinese Arithmetic', 'Surprise! You're Dead!', 'RV', 'Evidence', and 'Naked in Front of the Computer', but they are just five examples of the diversity the band has continually possessed, and it isn't surprising that for every rock band out there that have been influenced by Metallica, Iron Maiden, the Beatles, or Nirvana, there is a band who owes a debt of gratitude to Faith No More. Despite the tension, the fall-outs, the line-up changes, the on and off-stage antics, Faith just about managed to keep it together to make a decent career for themselves, where all they wanted to do was make music, tour globally, and have a lot of fun. Anything else that came with it was an added bonus.

Billy Gould said it perfectly during an interview with *Metal Hammer* magazine around the time of the release of *King for a Day... Fool for a Lifetime*, when looking back at Faith's modus operandi, and I think this extended quote is the perfect way to end this book:

You can look back and rack up your gold records on the wall and it doesn't mean a fucking thing if you know that at some point, you had to pretend to be someone you weren't. Faith No More, for all the huge crowds we played to, for all the albums we sold, for all the acclaim we got – we really didn't behave like or believe in the same things that a rock band was supposed to. I don't recall money or 'business' shit ever getting talked about. I don't recall arguments about anything but the music and that was just the way we made music.

To be able to keep that focus, to see through the shit and try and gain your immortality through music – that's something that I think we stuck to and never lost sight of. I'm totally proud of that, totally proud that I was part of something that never compromised and never took the easy way. That's a rarity in music, full stop.

Thank you for reading.

Matt Karpe

Bibliography

Books

Harte, A., *Small Victories: The True Story of Faith No More* (Jawbone Press, 2018)

Websites

allmusic.com
discogs.com
fnmfollowers.com
fnmlive.com
kerrang.com
loudersound.com
loudwire.com
nme.com
revolvermag.com
rollingstone.com
songfacts.com
wikipedia.com

Magazines

Kerrang!
Metal Hammer

On Track series
Allman Brothers Band – Andrew Wild
978-1-78952-252-5
Tori Amos – Lisa Torem 978-1-78952-142-9
Asia – Peter Braidis 978-1-78952-099-6
Badfinger – Robert Day-Webb
978-1-878952-176-4
Barclay James Harvest –
Keith and Monica Domone 978-1-78952-067-5
The Beatles – Andrew Wild 978-1-78952-009-5
The Beatles Solo 1969-1980 – Andrew Wild
978-1-78952-030-9
Blue Oyster Cult – Jacob Holm-Lupo
978-1-78952-007-1
Blur – Matt Bishop 978-178952-164-1
Marc Bolan and T.Rex – Peter Gallagher
978-1-78952-124-5
Kate Bush – Bill Thomas 978-1-78952-097-2
Camel – Hamish Kuzminski 978-1-78952-040-8
Captain Beefheart – Opher Goodwin
978-1-78952-235-8
Caravan – Andy Boot 978-1-78952-127-6
Cardiacs – Eric Benac 978-1-78952-131-3
Nick Cave and The Bad Seeds –
Dominic Sanderson 978-1-78952-240-2
Eric Clapton Solo – Andrew Wild
978-1-78952-141-2
The Clash – Nick Assirati 978-1-78952-077-4
Crosby, Stills and Nash – Andrew Wild
978-1-78952-039-2
Creedence Clearwater Revival –
Tony Thompson 978-178952-237-2
The Damned – Morgan Brown
978-1-78952-136-8
Deep Purple and Rainbow 1968-79 –
Steve Pilkington 978-1-78952-002-6
Dire Straits – Andrew Wild 978-1-78952-044-6
The Doors – Tony Thompson
978-1-78952-137-5
Dream Theater – Jordan Blum
978-1-78952-050-7
Electric Light Orchestra – Barry Delve
978-1-78952-152-8
Elvis Costello and The Attractions –
Georg Purvis 978-1-78952-129-0
Emerson Lake and Palmer – Mike Goode
978-1-78952-000-2
Fairport Convention – Kevan Furbank
978-1-78952-051-4
Peter Gabriel – Graeme Scarfe
978-1-78952-138-2
Genesis – Stuart MacFarlane 978-1-78952-005-7
Gentle Giant – Gary Steel 978-1-78952-058-3
Gong – Kevan Furbank 978-1-78952-082-8
Hall and Oates – Ian Abrahams
978-1-78952-167-2
Hawkwind – Duncan Harris 978-1-78952-052-1
Peter Hammill – Richard Rees Jones
978-1-78952-163-4
Roy Harper – Opher Goodwin
978-1-78952-130-6

Jimi Hendrix – Emma Stott 978-1-78952-175-7
The Hollies – Andrew Darlington
978-1-78952-159-7
The Human League and The Sheffield Scene –
Andrew Darlington 978-1-78952-186-3
Iron Maiden – Steve Pilkington
978-1-78952-061-3
Jefferson Airplane – Richard Butterworth
978-1-78952-143-6
Jethro Tull – Jordan Blum 978-1-78952-016-3
Elton John in the 1970s – Peter Kearns
978-1-78952-034-7
The Incredible String Band – Tim Moon
978-1-78952-107-8
Iron Maiden – Steve Pilkington
978-1-78952-061-3
Joe Jackson – Richard James 978-1-78952-189-4
Billy Joel – Lisa Torem 978-1-78952-183-2
Judas Priest – John Tucker 978-1-78952-018-7
Kansas – Kevin Cummings 978-1-78952-057-6
The Kinks – Martin Hutchinson
978-1-78952-172-6
Korn – Matt Karpe 978-1-78952-153-5
Led Zeppelin – Steve Pilkington
978-1-78952-151-1
Level 42 – Matt Philips 978-1-78952-102-3
Little Feat – Georg Purvis - 978-1-78952-168-9
Aimee Mann – Jez Rowden 978-1-78952-036-1
Joni Mitchell – Peter Kearns 978-1-78952-081-1
The Moody Blues – Geoffrey Feakes
978-1-78952-042-2
Motorhead – Duncan Harris 978-1-78952-173-3
Mike Oldfield – Ryan Yard 978-1-78952-060-6
Laura Nyro – Philip Ward 978-1-78952-182-5
Opeth – Jordan Blum 978-1-78-952-166-5
Pearl Jam – Ben L. Connor 978-1-78952-188-7
Tom Petty – Richard James 978-1-78952-128-3
Pink Floyd – Richard Butterworth
978-1-78952-242-6
Porcupine Tree – Nick Holmes
978-1-78952-144-3
Queen – Andrew Wild 978-1-78952-003-3
Radiohead – William Allen 978-1-78952-149-8
Rancid – Paul Matts 989-1-78952-187-0
Renaissance – David Detmer
978-1-78952-062-0
The Rolling Stones 1963-80 – Steve Pilkington
978-1-78952-017-0
The Smiths and Morrissey –
Tommy Gunnarsson 978-1-78952-140-5
Status Quo the Frantic Four Years –
Richard James 978-1-78952-160-3
Steely Dan – Jez Rowden 978-1-78952-043-9
Steve Hackett – Geoffrey Feakes
978-1-78952-098-9
Thin Lizzy – Graeme Stroud 978-1-78952-064-4
Tool – Matt Karpe 978-1-78952-234-1
Toto – Jacob Holm-Lupo 978-1-78952-019-4
U2 – Eoghan Lyng 978-1-78952-078-1
UFO – Richard James 978-1-78952-073-6
The Who – Geoffrey Feakes 978-1-78952-076-7

Roy Wood and the Move – James R Turner
978-1-78952-008-8
Stackridge – Alan Draper 978-1-78952-232-7
Van Der Graaf Generator – Dan Coffey
978-1-78952-031-6
Yes – Stephen Lambe 978-1-78952-001-9
Frank Zappa 1966 to 1979 – Eric Benac
978-1-78952-033-0
Warren Zevon – Peter Gallagher
978-1-78952-170-2
10CC – Peter Kearns 978-1-78952-054-5

Decades Series

The Bee Gees in the 1960s –
Andrew Mon Hughes et al 978-1-78952-148-1
The Bee Gees in the 1970s –
Andrew Mon Hughes et al 978-1-78952-179-5
Black Sabbath in the 1970s – Chris Sutton
978-1-78952-171-9
Britpop – Peter Richard Adams and Matt Pooler
978-1-78952-169-6
Phil Collins in the 1980s – Andrew Wild
978-1-78952-185-6
Alice Cooper in the 1970s – Chris Sutton
978-1-78952-104-7
Curved Air in the 1970s – Laura Shenton
978-1-78952-069-9
Donovan in the 1960s – Jeff Fitzgerald
978-1-78952-233-4
Bob Dylan in the 1980s – Don Klees
978-1-78952-157-3
Brian Eno in the 1970s – Gary Parsons
978-1-78952-239-6
Faith No More in the 1990s – Matt Karpe
978-1-78952-250-1
Fleetwood Mac in the 1970s – Andrew Wild
978-1-78952-105-4
Focus in the 1970s – Stephen Lambe
978-1-78952-079-8
Free and Bad Company in the 1970s –
John Van der Kiste 978-1-78952-178-8
Genesis in the 1970s – Bill Thomas
978178952-146-7
George Harrison in the 1970s – Eoghan Lyng
978-1-78952-174-0
Kiss in the 1970s – Peter Gallagher
978-1-78952-246-4
Marillion in the 1980s – Nathaniel Webb
978-1-78952-065-1
Van Morrison in the 1970s – 978-1-78952-241-9
Mott the Hoople and Ian Hunter in the 1970s –
John Van der Kiste 978-1-78-952-162-7
Pink Floyd In The 1970s – Georg Purvis
978-1-78952-072-9
Suzi Quatro in the 1970s – Darren Johnson
978-1-78952-236-5
Roxy Music in the 1970s – Dave Thompson
978-1-78952-180-1
Status Quo in the 1980s – Greg Harper
978-1-78952-244-0

Tangerine Dream in the 1970s –
Stephen Palmer 978-1-78952-161-0
Tears For Fears – Paul Clark 978-178952-238-9
The Sweet in the 1970s – Darren Johnson
978-1-78952-139-9
Uriah Heep in the 1970s – Steve Pilkington
978-1-78952-103-0
Van der Graaf Generator in the 1970s –
Steve Pilkington 978-1-78952-245-7
Yes in the 1980s – Stephen Lambe with
David Watkinson 978-1-78952-125-2

On Screen series

Carry On… – Stephen Lambe
978-1-78952-004-0
David Cronenberg – Patrick Chapman
978-1-78952-071-2
Doctor Who: The David Tennant Years –
Jamie Hailstone 978-1-78952-066-8
James Bond – Andrew Wild –
978-1-78952-010-1
Monty Python – Steve Pilkington
978-1-78952-047-7
Seinfeld Seasons 1 to 5 – Stephen Lambe
978-1-78952-012-5

Other Books

1967: A Year In Psychedelic Rock
978-1-78952-155-9
1970: A Year In Rock – John Van der Kiste
978-1-78952-147-4
1973: The Golden Year of Progressive Rock
978-1-78952-165-8
Babysitting A Band On The Rocks –
G.D. Praetorius 978-1-78952-106-1
Eric Clapton Sessions – Andrew Wild
978-1-78952-177-1
Derek Taylor: For Your Radioactive Children –
Andrew Darlington 978-1-78952-038-5
The Golden Road: The Recording History of
The Grateful Dead – John Kilbride
978-1-78952-156-6
Iggy and The Stooges On Stage 1967-1974 –
Per Nilsen 978-1-78952-101-6
Jon Anderson and the Warriors – the road to
Yes – David Watkinson 978-1-78952-059-0
Misty: The Music of Johnny Mathis –
Jakob Baekgaard 978-1-78952-247-1
Nu Metal: A Definitive Guide – Matt Karpe
978-1-78952-063-7
Tommy Bolin: In and Out of Deep Purple –
Laura Shenton 978-1-78952-070-5
Maximum Darkness – Deke Leonard
978-1-78952-048-4
The Twang Dynasty – Deke Leonard
978-1-78952-049-1

and many more to come!